SEPTEMBER
2019

TO VIRGIL,

MY WISH
FIND A FEW "GOLD NUGGETS"
TO ELEVATE YOUR INVESTMENTS
WITH GODS' BLESSINGS

ASK THE MAILMAN

A Simple Plan of High-Yield Stock
Investing for Uncommon Wealth

david l. hawkins

WESTBOW
P R E S S®
A DIVISION OF THOMAS NELSON
& ZONDERVAN

WestBow Press books may be ordered through booksellers or by contacting:

WestBow Press
A Division of Thomas Nelson & Zondervan
1663 Liberty Drive
Bloomington, IN 47403
www.westbowpress.com
1 (866) 928-1240

Scripture taken from The Living Bible, copyright © 1971 by Tyndale House Foundation. Used by permission of Tyndale House Publishers Inc., Carol Stream, Illinois 60188. All rights reserved. The Living Bible, TLB, and the The Living Bible logo are registered trademarks of Tyndale House Publishers.

ISBN: 978-1-9736-6090-3 (sc)
ISBN: 978-1-9736-6089-7 (e)

Library of Congress Control Number: 2019906644

Printed in China.

WestBow Press rev. date: 6/19/2019

Dedication

In loving memory of Fletcher Thomas ("Tom") and Dorothy Hawkins. It was parenting that set the gold standards for their four children to live by. They told us to make as many mistakes as were necessary for us to learn from and then share our experiences so that others may benefit from our roadblocks. Lack of money was not a curse to our family; it was an exercise in resourcefulness and ingenuity. Some of our family's happiest routines were midday dinners on Sundays. Laughter was always on the menu, and the meal was lovingly selected to please—and it could be stretched out for a few meals the rest of the week.

They said, "Do what you say you are going to do," "Treat others the way you want to be treated," "If you always tell the truth, then your story will always be the same," and "Always invite God to the dinner table." Our parents wanted us to embrace these family's values and make them part of our core values. I hope you will feel the blessings my parents wanted to pass on to us as well as others through God.

Preface

Human nature, for the most part, is very predictable. As teenagers, we thought we knew everything there was to know. We took foolish dares and did foolish stunts that could have harmed or even killed us, and we thought nothing of it. In fact, we were indignant if our intelligence was challenged. Then we went into our settling down years, got married, had kids, and professed how stupid and reckless we were in our youth—and how we didn't want our children to be as stupid as we were.

Then you get to the point in life when things are nearing completion. The kids are grown and out of the house. They might even be married and have kids of their own. One day, you start looking back on your life and you think, *Is this all there is?* or *This has been great—I have enjoyed the trip.*

Ask the Mailman came into being because I have enjoyed my journey, and I want to continue the exciting, trailblazing paths I have uncovered, gleaned, and refined. Hopefully, readers might have a little easier journey. We spend most of our lives trying to gather, gain ground, and get ahead. Many of us are so focused on that carrot dangling in front of us that we barely notice the beautiful scenery around us.

One of the best parts of life is when we get a chance to give back, and it can come in many forms. *Ask the Mailman* is one of the ways I want to contribute to those who are searching for ways to master their own financial destinies. Read the examples in this book, apply them, master a balanced and prosperous financial model, and pass it on to others.

Acknowledgments

I have never done anything worthwhile without the help of others. Writing this book has added a dimension to my life that is indescribable. This part of my book gives me great joy because I can share with the world all the people who helped me get this book written.

My team starts with Cheryl Leyland. She drafted my chicken scratches into a readable format that could be edited (I can't type to save my life—and don't ask me to text you a message). Cheryl has multiple tasks in our design firm as an associate designer and put this book into a readable format for the first time.

Dr. Mary Jo Fresch, a professor emeritus of education at Ohio State University, has lectured around the world and written more than twenty books. She structured my manuscript and edited it so that it could be submitted for publishing.

Anita Marron is a talented graphic artist who has worked with our design firm for many years in multiple capacities. She directed the setup of the graphics for this book and added her talent to the final look.

Anthony Panici is my business coordinator for all our corporate holdings and is essentially my right hand when it comes to letting me know what is happening with my interests.

He has kept me on track with my responsibilities for getting our book published, and his involvement will be ongoing.

George Chaney is one of my closest colleagues and a dear friend. He, and I have bantered back and forth many times, and he added his "ether humor" to soften the subject for the reader, which adds to the enjoyability of the book.

Wendy Geonis—my wife, confidante, and biggest cheerleader—was sitting next to me in the Gulf of Mexico when I got the revelation to recreate my investment journey on paper and share it with anyone who wanted a helping hand in growing their money.

Tom and Dorothy Hawkins (Dad and Mom) showed relentless patience in raising their most incorrigible child of the four. They were constantly guiding and redirecting me to a path of acceptable behavior. They were always sure God had blessed each of their children with talents that would sustain each of them for life's journey—they just weren't sure if I would live to reach adulthood. My parents' love, understanding, and teaching us that all good things in our lives come from God were the most important contributions to this book.

Author's Note

I did not want to make my investments my career, but I was willing to put enough effort into it so that I could have a retirement account that was worth something and would yield a bounty that could afford me the flexibility to do whatever I wanted in retirement. A secure retirement through my investment became my mission. For at least two hours every morning, my father, and I started looking for investments that could net us high returns.

When you maximize the resources available to you, dig for ways to grow your money without tremendous risk, and systematically invest more in the stock market, you can achieve high returns. I know that's possible because I have done it—all without paying exorbitant fees to a money manager claiming to look out for your best interests, I share the strategies that have worked for me— as well as the ones that haven't—in this do-it-yourself guide to managing investments. The result will be overwhelming.

Pay particular attention to investing for income, noting that if you have a $60,000 investment that pays you $1,000 a month ($12,000 annually), it will take only five years to get your money back. I encourage you to use this simple plan for achieving uncommon wealth by investing in high-yield stocks and start making your cash work for you and your family with the guidance in Ask the Mailman.

Contents

Part 4: Wait... There's More (Aww... Come On)

Part 5: Want More... Give More!

PART 1

A Sling Shot Starts The Journey

1

10¢ Is A Lot Of Money...
If You Don't Have It

"The best way to teach your children about money is to not have any." That was one of many proverbs I heard while growing up. There are thousands of stories like mine across this country, and many are more dynamic and dramatic. This is not really a rags-to-riches story. It is about the quest to maximize all the resources available to you, dig for ways to advance your money safely—without tremendous risk—and systematically and confidently increase your invested money, regardless of the climate of the stock market.

Many before me have been fortunate enough to carve out their own successful paths. This book is fulfilling my need to help others find a way to get their dreams within reach, persevere, and hit their goals. My real driving force is to share the formulas that have maximized my investment efforts. There are probably as many different definitions of dreams as there are people who are trying to make them a reality.

I would venture to say that most people's dreams in some way, shape, or form are connected to money, and there are probably just as many definitions of what part money plays in their dreams. For me, money has been the sharpest, most versatile tool you can have in your toolbox. A good carpenter always has a wide variety of sharp tools to handle any task at hand, and that is what you should have to tackle the daily challenges and build your dreams. I will share things that have helped me over time and made the journey smoother and more interesting, exciting, and fun.

The principles I have used to increase my investments have been in place since the beginning of time. Laws of mathematics, laws of the universe, and principles brought to light by reading other investors' stories and adapting ideas have shaped my investment model. I have applied the principle of charity, knowing that all things come from God, and sharing knowledge with others as one of many ways to help His cause.

Why buy stocks... but not just any stocks

The first time I ever heard about stocks, mutual funds, and investing I was in junior high school. I was probably thirteen years old. My father was a mailman in the sixties, and he would bring home day-old *Wall Street Journals* that were saved for him by one of the residents on his delivery route. Yesterday's paper—old information. He was so hungry for that information but had no money to spend on that daily paper. He found a way to get what would help him in the most painless manner he could.

Here's where I'm supposed to explain that we were poor. I don't think my siblings or I thought we were poor until we were on our own and looked back at our childhood. When my mother passed away, I was compelled to write a reflection of my mother's impact on my life. It was one of the easiest things I ever done. It just flowed.

At her memorial service, I shared a vivid recollection of the time I asked her for a dime so that I could go to our local five-and-dime store to buy a slingshot.

She told me no.

I replied, "But it is only ten cents."

She replied, "David, ten cents is a lot of money if you don't have it, isn't it?"

Wow! Ten cents or a million dollars—they are the same if you don't have them. Even though I was only six years old, I can remember it like it was yesterday. At six years old, I got a startling lesson on what money was about.

A "hardworking family," "trying to make ends meet," "work smarter, not harder" and a few other clichés were the driving forces that revealed to my father, through his studies of the *Wall Street Journal,* a few stocks that he thought made sense. He was looking for solid companies that paid a dividend. His first investment was an oil stock that paid 11 percent. It was also a preferred stock, not the common stock, which he explained to me. If there were any dividends to be paid, the preferred stockholders got the payout first.

That little tidbit—along with a few others—was my introduction into boring chatter from my father about stocks. He proceeded to make extra money and prompt me to join him in the investment world. He hounded me to take some of my money from cutting grass and shoveling snow and invest into his preselected mutual fund, and I caved.

I think I did it just to keep him quiet (it didn't work). I bought ten shares of his selected mutual fund, at about $21 per share, which paid about 8 percent annually. In turn, it netted me a check once a year for about $16. At first, I watched the fund's activity in that day-old paper. It moved up and down, which was not very exciting for a teenager. It was almost like watching paint dry.

Over time, the fund went down to about seven dollars. When I pointed this out to my father, he told me that I had a great buying opportunity before me. I told my father that it would have been better to buy a new bike instead of losing money in the stock market. I could have a lot more fun and a bike in the garage instead of a piece of paper showing stock ownership and not really knowing what happened to that money.

I thought that was pretty sound wisdom for a fourteen-year-old. Knowing what I know now, it is clear that much of our society feels the same way about investing in the stock market. If I had only listened to my father and stuck with his original plan and advice! I should have kept it going. Instead, I gave up on any kind of securities investments.

In 1980, President Ronald Reagan initiated personal

individual retirement accounts, which are better known as IRAs. I was all over that! Just graduating from college and having no luck landing the type of job I wanted, I had a burning desire to not work all my life and have nothing to show for it.

The other steering force that was eating at me was that my father, being a letter carrier for more than sixteen years, had enough of a job battling the elements, winter, summer, rain, shine and sticking little pieces of paper in tin boxes—many times up flights of stairs for people who wouldn't shovel the snow.

He quit his job.

The look of horror on my mother's face will be etched in my mind forever, and on top of that, he took his pension of sixteen years—plus four years from the military—in a lump sum payout of $3,000. I was with him when he opened the check that came in the mail.

When he showed it to me, I thought, *So little money for such hard work*.

Although he never said it, I know he felt the same way. Instead of getting bitter about it, he got busy using that seed money to build his future. For the next several years, he was very aggressive about finding ways to make that pension check grow through investing in the stock market.

At the same time, I was eagerly maxing out my personal IRA to the limit allowed by law and trying to put money aside for emergencies—of, which there seemed to be more of than calm times.

Our investment paths did not cross again for probably the next ten years, which was due to a failed marriage and lack of funds on my part. I found myself right back where I started life:

my parent's home. I was very painfully self-employed, trying to build a business with only $1,100 in my business checking account. I could have asked for half of all our assets, but I didn't. There was only one reason I refused to fight for what was rightfully mine by law: my son. I did not want him to see his parents fighting over money or things. It was painful enough having parents uproot you without worrying about what was going to happen to your life. The lack of money was not worth the additional pain that would have been inflicted on him.

I was healthy, I had worked, and I had loving parents who understood and supported me. As it turns out, that seeming disaster became a huge blessing. Here's where I mention another one of those proverbs I heard at the dining table growing up: "God will never close the door on you without giving you a window to climb out of."

After a couple of weeks of licking my wounds, I realized I couldn't dwell on self-pity. I had responsibilities, a young son, contracts with clients, and meager assets to try to keep things moving forward. All things happen for a reason—some of them by our own hand and others unexplained. What happened next was very much a turning point in my investment journey.

My father, and I were both early risers. Every morning, he would already be up having a cup of coffee, waiting for the *Wall Street Journal*, which arrived promptly on his front porch at four o'clock. Many times, when I would get up, he would pour me the morning eye-opener and ask me to fire up the computer and get him some info on stocks that he had already scoped out for potential purchase.

We would do this every morning before heading out to work. It became a ritual for us. We didn't always agree on the companies to purchase. For whatever reason, he would like a stock I didn't care for it, but that was okay. He would buy it, and then we would watch it every day along with all the other holdings we had. We would share news about the company's movement in the market. I was still pretty heavily invested into mutual funds, which were much easier to look at and understand.

I was hungry for more in-depth information about investing than the daily paper provided, and Warren Buffett's name was always being thrown around in the *Wall Street Journal*. The things being said about him were so appealing. For all his wealth, he still lived in his first house in Omaha, Nebraska, drove himself to work in an older car, and had no computer to help with his stock research. He almost sounded like a bit of a recluse.

I bought a book about Warren Buffett. My selection, *Of Permanent Value*, was a huge book: 871 pages and 157 chapters! I thought it was going to be like reading the dictionary, but the book described the investment icon very well and in detail. It explained how he approached acquiring stock and companies for his portfolio and his benchmark for the acquisitions he made. Buffett wants a 20 percent return on investment (ROI). How can he do that?

On top of that, whenever he bought an entire company that met his standard profile for growth rate and strength, he kept everything running just as it was before he bought it. His one exception was that all profits were sent to him for investment use. It was an amazing investment plan.

It didn't take long after reading the philosophies of the world's greatest investor to inspire me to develop a philosophy of my own. I would be able to reach, compare, evaluate, implement, and, most importantly, stick to the plan. I would not just mimic Warren Buffett's plan. He digs so deeply and spends so much time poring over charts and reports. If I took his approach, there would be no time for my current daytime obligations. That could be a good thing if your investments are so large that it is your job, but I was light years away from that.

Many investors track Warren's activities and buy what he buys. There is nothing wrong with that, but it also takes a lot of time and effort to shadow his investments. The simplest way to follow in his footsteps is to buy Berkshire Hathaway stock, but as a neophyte investor, I didn't fully understand the rules of percentages. I was totally intimidated by the sheer cost of Berkshire Hathaway's stock (both A and B).

I finally came away with the inspiration to create an investment model that I could handle myself. I thought 20 percent ROI was just off the chart—too aggressive—thinking that if I set goals too high and never got close to them, I'd get discouraged and quit. If you see progress, you get encouraged and keep trying. That's our nature. I was pumped up and set my goals at 15 percent ROI.

Looking at what I was currently invested in revealed I wasn't doing too bad at an average of about 8–9 percent. How was I going to make up that extra 6–7 percent? That is where the challenge really starts. It really isn't difficult to get an 8 percent ROI if you want to just dump your investments into mutual funds and let it ride.

You could also go to any of the thousands of investment planners, tell them your goals, and see if they can fulfill your criteria. I tried that. And here is what happened. I met with a financial planner who was recommended by a close friend I totally trusted. I met with this young man, who was quite a bit younger than me and had a nice client base of more than three hundred clients. Not too big, not too small. He handled all his accounts personally, and he was very thorough in finding out my comfort level for risk, the return I was looking for, and all the other long-term goals. We discussed how he would approach the earnings and invest them back into the holdings.

When I felt that everything could work, I asked him the uncomfortable question: "How do you get compensated for handling my account?"

He probably wasn't sure I had heard him correctly.

He repeated his statement, and I came back to him with a crystal clear question: "Just so I am sure I understand you, if my account doesn't earn any dividends, then you don't get paid, correct?"

He affirmed his 1.5 percent fee and told me that he "handles everything."

This will work, I thought. I signed up with his firm, signed the papers to transfer all my investments to his firm, and sat down with him to finalize the investment allocations. I felt what I had just put in place would give me the freedom from the anxiety from having to figure out what to do with my money. I could sit back and watch my account grow like a sunflower. I could become a couch potato investor.

When I got the statement of my account, it was nothing shocking. It merely showed the account opening cash balance. However, the next month, I was stunned. My statement revealed that I had earned 1 percent for the month—12 percent annually. That was excellent in the very first month, but what was not so great were the charges deducted from my account. His fee was 1.5 percent all right, but it was 1.5 percent of the entire account value, not 1.5 percent of my 1 percent earnings, as he professed.

The next day, I made an appointment with him to close my account. I didn't really want to hear any explanations of misunderstanding or excuses. He totally misled me about fees. Period.

Leaving his office, I thought, *How many of those three hundred clients invested with him were misled—or are they okay with his fees?* They are giving up 18 percent of their account value each year. Those thoughts led me to one of my father's sayings: "No one will look after your money like you do."

From that point on, I have had total control and self-directed all my investments. Results can be good or bad, but I have nobody else to blame or praise for the results.

All this searching for the investment panacea led me right back to my childhood kitchen table, which was where I had my very first exposure to investing. Searching for gold nuggets in a vast sea of mutual funds and stocks always took time and research, but it always netted a catch or something to look into.

Warren Buffett's benchmarks were high, I realized, because all his diligence is really hard work. That was the reason he has been able to consistently net 20 percent earnings on his investments. I realized that another one of life's proverbs was in place: "Anything worthwhile requires work and effort and will take time to develop."

I did not want to make my investments my career, but I was willing to put enough effort into it so that I could have a retirement account that was worth something and would yield a bounty that could afford me the flexibility to do whatever I wanted in retirement. A secure retirement through my investment became my mission. For at least two hours every morning, my father, and I started looking for investments that could net us high returns.

Let's put this effort into a measurement that everyone understands: Two men working two hours a day, five days a week, equals twenty man hours of effort. Annually, that is 1,040 hours of work. I equate this effort to early prospectors panning for gold during the California gold rush. Once you have what you are looking for it, is exhilarating. You become supercharged, and your quest becomes so meaningful that you look forward to the task. I can imagine what those prospectors felt like when a gold nugget showed up in the pan—and knowing it is out there waiting to be uncovered, discovered, and harvested. It is yours for the taking.

Once we started finding these high-yield investments, we had to dig into the information about the newfound treasures. We had to sort the good ones from the not-so-good ones and then select the best, based on the standards we wanted. It became clear to me that I needed to shift my selection of investments from mutual funds to stocks. (This philosophy will be touched on in chapters ahead).

One of my major investments was in a mutual fund that was actually founded by a man in my hometown. He was a pension administrator with one of the large rubber companies and decided to go out on his own and start an investment fund. Like many mutual funds in the late nineties, it was doing very well. The fund was approaching its historical all-time high of about $100 per share, which was really remarkable, considering where it was when I first bought into it.

I clearly remember the morning the *Wall Street Journal* confirmed that this particular mutual fund hit its all-time high. A very strange feeling came over me; it was time to sell this holding. If I did not take advantage of the fund's all-time high, I might never see it as high again. I shared my thoughts with my father, and without a moment's hesitation, he said, "Take the money and run."

This is the one part of investing where I see how many people get the sensation that investing in the stock market is a lot like gambling. You are letting your money ride, using the house's money, or having a large amount of money evaporate. There are many similarities, and I have made investments with results that made me feel as sickly as if I had just left as a loser at the blackjack table.

The stock market historically has made many people wealthy and many people broke, but someone has always made money using their investment strategy. Even during and right after the stock market crash of 1929, investors made money because their plans were based on what was happening in the market at the time of the crash. The single worst thing that a self-directed investor can do is panic.

The worst thing you can do is panic. How many times has

someone said that to you? If you're in an accident—don't panic. If someone is having a heart attack, don't panic. This is not to say panicking about your money is the same as panicking when your life—or the life of someone you love—is in danger. The point is to stay calm, take a deep breath, and see what action needs to be taken. Think clearly.

The best thing to do in all these situations is have a plan: formulate the steps you need to take, do a practice run, and stick to your plan. Once you start watching what the market does on a daily basis, you will start to notice trends that move the market. News releases usually cause a little movement up and down, which causes somebody to react either positively or negatively—and that normally changes daily. When there is a sell-off, somebody is causing panic, which triggers others to sell, and so on and so on. There are much larger, more complex elements in stock market trends that I don't want to touch on or even have any interest in. I want a simple plan that can pay on your investment even in a down market.

I just sold my largest mutual fund, which had jumped to four times what I paid for it. That was great, but what would I do with that money to keep it growing? I formulated a plan based on the inspiration that I had gotten from Warren Buffett's biography and added my guidelines to create a plan that could help me grow my retirement investments. My plan was to find quality investments that paid an annual dividend of 15 percent. That was my benchmark.

I was ready to put my new investment plan into action using a large cache of cash to invest (well, it was large for me). I had several stocks selected, and I was ready to pull the trigger.

Here comes another saying from my mother: "David, that money must be burning a hole in your pocket."

I was eager to get that money back into the market and start engaging my newly developed philosophy. I had a list of issues I was interested in getting into my portfolio. I wanted to start with a strong, stable, blue chip stock, and I wanted one that paid more than 6 percent as a dividend. I did more in-depth investigating and created a short list of my favorites to start with and divided the amount of money I had to invest.

I had six stocks, and I allocated 40 percent of the money on the strongest issue, 20 percent on the next issue, 15 percent on the next two issues—at 10 percent each—and 5 percent for the highest-yielding stock, which was also the most volatile. "Most volatile" doesn't necessarily mean the riskiest. It just moves around a lot, has ups and downs, and is not consistent. It looked promising, and I was cautiously optimistic.

I felt ready to test the waters, which is another Warren Buffett trick. He buys one hundred shares of a company he is interested in to get their annual report. This is his way of seeing who is running the company, who is controlling where his money is going, and what will they do with it.

Before I made my purchases, I "back-tested" the ROI. I calculated the dividends for each issue annually and divided it by twelve to see what I would be earning monthly. This wasn't completely accurate because a few of the stocks only paid quarterly, which made the monthly amount more of an average, which was good enough for forecasting.

To my surprise, this block of money was going to net me close to 18 percent annually. When I averaged it in with the other investments, it brought it down to less than 12 percent annually. It was a respectable return on investment by anyone's standards—except maybe Warren Buffett's. Coming up with a strategy was exciting, and the plan would generate high yields to help make my IRA grow faster. If it was going to work, I was close to achieving what Warren Buffett was doing at Berkshire Hathaway. It was making my head swell.

Over the next several weeks, my father and I watched the newest purchases through several dividend cycles, which confirmed our research was on target with the goals I set. The next step was to sell off the rest of my mutual funds and convert them to my new plan of high-yield stocks. Fortunately, at the time, selling was good. Things were all higher than when I purchased them, and there would be additional money to reinvest.

However, I failed to realize that when you sell in an up market, the chances are very good that the next stock you buy will also be up. There are no bargain-basement deals, but you can hold onto your cash, wait for a deal, and then jump in. That is what investment advisors call "timing the market," but it rarely has been something I can take the time to do. Your money, sitting on the sidelines, is not earning the 1.5 percent monthly it would be earning if you were in at the higher price.

Do the math to see what will net you the most return. For me, the monthly income is the best. I would rather have that than a bargain on price. With that thinking in mind, I made a leap of faith and liquidated the rest of my mutual funds. For the second time, I had a cache of cash to do something with, but there was less uncertainty about what to do with it and how to go about it. After reviewing all the facts and doing the math, I felt the risk was less than the reward. Selling my holdings at a high point also meant that if I was buying new positions, I was buying on the high side as well. I was more focused on the monthly and quarterly return than the cost of the stock.

With high yields that are consistent, it is easy to calculate how quickly your investment pays you back. If you have a $60,000 investment that pays you $1,000 a month ($12,000 annually), it will take only five years to get your money back on your investment ($60,000 ÷ $12,000 = 5). That is assuming that nothing changes or moves.

I can say with pretty much certainty that a perfect formula will not happen, but it can pay out better whether it is in dividend payout or an increase in the share price. A budget is the closest you will be able to forecast the future of your investments. Another quick formula to help you forecast your earnings is the rule of 72. This rule is a snapshot of how your money grows based on the interest you are earning. So if you are earning 8 percent interest, divide it into 72 (72 ÷ 8 = 9) the quotient will tell you how many years it will take for your money to double in value.

If you have $50,000 earning 8 percent interest, it will take nine years for it to become $100,000. Now depending on your mind-set, outlook on life, goals, and ambitions, you will say, "Wow! It will only take nine years for that money to earn another $50,000 if I just let it ride," or "Wow! I don't know if I can wait that long for my money to earn another $50,000."

If you asked one hundred people which of those two views would be closest to their comfort level on investing, I bet the majority would be totally content to sit back with 8 percent earnings and just let it ride. There is nothing wrong with letting your money accumulate and grow at 8 percent, but you will not be able to get a consistent high rate where you can sit back and let things ride.

There have been times when conditions were such that I could take advantage of high returns. High returns are still available, but they are not as visible as a ripe apple easily spotted and picked. I don't know that we will ever see passbook savings or certificates of deposits with high interest rates again. If they do rise, rates for investment returns will also rise.

When money goes into bank accounts instead of the stock market, people settle for less ROI since it is safer and easier to get their hands on, resulting in more nights of peaceful sleep. It is competition for your discretionary income, the money you have left after you pay all your bills. (A contribution to a retirement account should be part of your monthly bills and should not come out of your discretionary income).

People will generally take the path of least resistance. It is one of the many laws of our universe. Water finds the easiest path all on its own, but we can channel water to flow the way we want it to go with a little effort. It can be guided to flow into a pool that will grow. Human nature is pretty simple and easy to figure out. There will always be people who are satisfied with simple and easy, little, or no extra effort. They have no goals.

The overachievers are never satisfied with normal or average and always want more. They want to hit or exceed their goals. They can be obsessed with their goals to the point of making themselves neurotic. (I've never met an obsessive underachiever). I have found an investment balance somewhere in between my local bank's savings account and Warren Buffett without losing sleep and still having a life.

No matter what investment path you choose—stocks, bonds, certificates of deposit, or a plain passbook savings account—there is an element in force that is universal. It is a mathematic principle. It is the greatest builder of wealth or the greatest anchor around your neck, depending on whether you are applying it to money you are earning or money you are paying debt off with. This phenomenon is called *compound interest*.

PART 2

Compound Interest

3

Those Who Understand It Earn It, Those Who Don't, Pay It

The very first time I was made aware of the magical principle known as compound interest was in, of all places, a sociology class during my freshman year of college. I could not even begin to tell you why this example ever came up in class. In fact, I wish I could find that textbook that I have stored away somewhere so that I could review the point the author was trying to make. Subsequently, I have seen similar examples of this story. Here is my paraphrased version of this tale:

Long ago, there was a kingdom where one of the king's subjects approached the king and proclaimed, "I can take your kingdom from you within one month by using a bowl of rice."

The king said, "Go on. How do you propose to take my kingdom from me by using a bowl of rice?"

The wise subject replied, "For the next month, starting with a bowl of rice on day one, then every day for the next month, double the amount each day."

The king thought this subject's challenge was absurd. "How can my kingdom be taken from me using a bowl of rice?" Foolishly, the king accepted this dare.

Here is how the king's subject took away his kingdom→

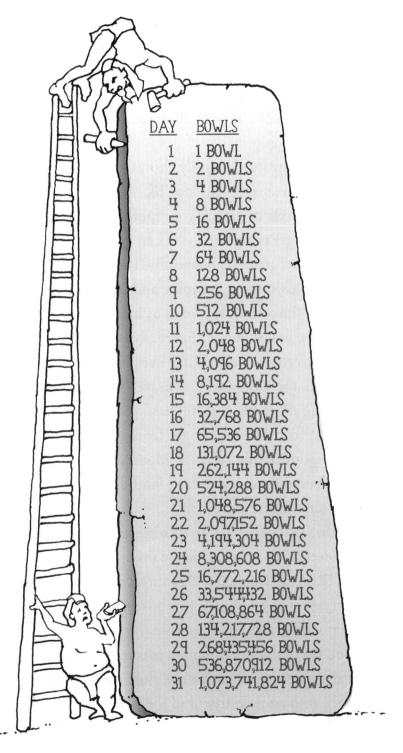

DAY	BOWLS
1	1 BOWL
2	2 BOWLS
3	4 BOWLS
4	8 BOWLS
5	16 BOWLS
6	32 BOWLS
7	64 BOWLS
8	128 BOWLS
9	256 BOWLS
10	512 BOWLS
11	1,024 BOWLS
12	2,048 BOWLS
13	4,096 BOWLS
14	8,192 BOWLS
15	16,384 BOWLS
16	32,768 BOWLS
17	65,536 BOWLS
18	131,072 BOWLS
19	262,144 BOWLS
20	524,288 BOWLS
21	1,048,576 BOWLS
22	2,097,152 BOWLS
23	4,194,304 BOWLS
24	8,308,608 BOWLS
25	16,772,216 BOWLS
26	33,544,132 BOWLS
27	67,108,864 BOWLS
28	134,217,728 BOWLS
29	268,435,456 BOWLS
30	536,870,912 BOWLS
31	1,073,741,824 BOWLS

By using 100 percent compound interest daily, a bowl of rice grew to more than five hundred million bowls of rice in thirty days. If there were thirty-one days in the month, the single bowl of rice grew to more than one billion bowls of rice. The mathematic laws, as with all the rules of our universe, are amazing and absolute.

This demonstration acutely shows the magnum force of compound interest once the snowball starts to pick up speed. Using the principle of having your money earn interest on the interest is the greatest force you can put into play to make your investments grow exponentially. This investment concept may, at first blush, seem complex and involved. It has some complexity to the overall approach by having to find high-yield investments to invest in, but that really is it.

Buy a stock that pays you cash every month or every three months. Take the cash and buy more. The very next month, you're getting more interest because you bought more stock with interest (dividends) you got from the previous month's interest. This principle can, and does, apply to many other forms of investments: real estate, land development, venture capitalization, the list can go on.

Anything that generates an income stream can get you into compound-earning mode. And isn't that the whole point of a fund? An IRA at retirement will be an income stream to sustain your lifestyle when you decide to stop working. Developers will invest in tracts of land and then construct rentable space to be leased out. Once the development is complete and the project is generating a positive cash flow, they have additional cash to put back into an investment of their own choice. This is an oversimplification of property development, but the money-stream principle is the same.

This wealth-building phenomena can just as easily work against you if you are loaded with consumer debt that is racking up interest on your unpaid principal. If you are making monthly payments that are not neutralizing the interest, that snowball is rolling over you.

As you can see by the bowl of rice example, it is much better to be earning compound interest than paying it. Consumer debt is probably one of the most destructive forces in our country, and by consumer debt, I mean credit cards. Credit cards in themselves are a wonderful tool, but if not used responsibly, they can be demonizing. (Credit card advantages will be discussed in future chapters).

My goal here is now to show how compound interest can generate wealth at an accelerated rate. I want to show some simple ways to take advantage of this fabulous element that can help you achieve the maximum for your saving and investing efforts. Here is my very simple plan→

1. Get Money

moneta arbor (money tree)

you

basket of moneta (money)

2. Buy something that Pays you back

← you

← moneta arbor sapling (baby money tree)

3. Keep Repeating Steps 1 And 2 !

Let's go through the steps to see how easy it can be to get compound interest working for you.

4

Get Money

"When you clean the fountain pick up the change."

How do most of us get money? Depending on your situation, it can be joyful or painful, but the majority of us "get money" by getting up and going to work to earn a living through gainful efforts. If you don't enjoy what you do to earn a living, please look for an alternate way. The journey should be just as joyful as the destination. If you can get paid for something that you love doing, you will improve all the energies in your life.

Most of us work forty to sixty hours per week. If work takes up fifty hours of our time per week, that is about 30 percent or one-third of hours in a seven-day week. That leaves about 70 percent of our hours left for us to do as we wish. Now you have 118 hours left. If you take out sleeping and commuting time, you will have about sixty hours per week to do whatever you want.

Some of those sixty hours per week could be used to get money. A second or part-time job can help get extra money. It really depends on how much you want to get money. Maybe you have a creative hobby or collect things to sell at a profit;

this could help you get money. Other ways to get money include using rebates, cash-back rewards, coupons, and gifts. Set that money aside to invest.

When my son was young, we would collect aluminum cans as we walked the family dog. We took the cans home, crushed them, added them to our own cans, and turned them in for cash. We acquired enough to buy twelve hundred-dollar savings bonds toward his college education. That equated to six hundred dollars in cash, which was not bad for picking up and saving trash.

There is always a way to get money. When I finished college, I worked full-time and went to school full-time. Every quarter, when tuition was due, I always found enough work doing something to pay it. The day I graduated, I went to pick up my diploma and paid off the last of my school bill, which was a whopping three hundred dollars.

Another way to get money is allocating the money you already have. When you empty your pockets at the end of the day, keep your loose change. When you have saved up a couple hundred bucks, put it into your investment plan. It will amaze you how quickly that money adds up.

5

Be Your Own Broker...
Open A Brokerage Account

To effectively trade securities online, you need to open an account with a brokerage firm with online trading services. They are all very similar in the services that will assist you in your trading situations and executing your trades. The fees they charge are now about $4.95 per trade. The fee is really the least concern of having your trading account with any of the big trading houses. The features of your account support your ability to make decisions on stocks you should be interested in.

No matter which firm you choose, you will get an account representative, and most likely, they will be located at an office close to wherever you live. Take advantage of this feature. You will have a live person to meet with and show you how to use the internet for trading and research. Your account representative will also show you their suggestions. Be openminded and listen to what they have to say with regard to how the market works. You may even like some of their approaches as a matter of diversification for your portfolio.

If you have them make any purchases on your behalf or by your instruction, you will pay a higher fee for those transactions—and a good account representative will tell you so. I personally have two accounts with different brokerage firms. The first one has all of our family's personal investment accounts; the other has all of our business investments. Both companies assign an account representative to my accounts. These representatives are important enough to me that I want a relationship with them should I need inside assistance with a problem.

One young man has been my account rep for almost fifteen years. He has moved up within the company, but he has become a trusted friend of our family. He understands my investment philosophy so completely that I have entrusted him to handle my finances should I have an untimely departure. Even though he is no longer my account rep within that company, we still talk and share ideas.

Find a good brokerage firm, build a relationship with your rep, and if you don't like the results or the way your account is handled, go to a different firm. It is your money, and they want your trades. Another important benefit of a brokerage account with a large firm is the research tools and rating systems for stocks you may be interested in purchasing. I find it interesting that each brokerage house has such different research tools and ways information is presented.

I use both account research materials for quite different reasons. The same information will come up in different ways. It really is a matter of preference. Both of my current account representatives periodically have wanted me to sit down with them to review my accounts, make sure I am happy with the company's service, and see if I'm still satisfied with my self-directed stock purchases. Although neither young stockbroker fully agrees with me or understands how I approach my investment selections, all three of us wholeheartedly agree on the importance of finding an investment plan that makes you feel comfortable and encourages you to save more because of positive results.

Once you have created an investment plan, stick to it! Don't panic and sell at a loss if the stock is paying you monthly or quarterly. There is no reason to sell because of a downturn in the market. As long as the dividends are coming in, a buying opportunity is around the corner.

Anyone in the financial world, investment world, banking world, or business world—large or small—will agree that cash is king. With cash, you can do anything. It is the sharpest, most versatile tool in your toolbox.

This acronym can help you remember a simple investment philosophy→

reate a saving investment plan that is comfortable for you. (It has to be one that will allow you to sleep at night.)

lways try to pay yourself first. (If you do this without fail, you soon will be able to have some of your monthly bills paid with investment earnings.)

tick to your plan! (Don't be a lemming and follow others off the cliff just because the market drops, which it will always do. It is not a reason to sell off.)

old on to the stocks that will keep on paying you to own them. (As long as a stock pays you the amount you are expecting every month or quarter, hold it in your portfolio.)

6

Buy Something That Pays You Back

For years, a passbook savings account was the way everyone put money into the neighborhood bank and earned a little bit of interest. Certificates of deposit (CDs) were popular among older people who were afraid of or didn't want anything to do with the stock market.

I have all my funds in either a bank checking account or a brokerage account with large investment companies. My brokerage accounts all also have check-writing capabilities so that I can write checks from the proceeds of my investments. Stocks are my preferred investment choice, specifically high-yielding stocks.

Most financial planners will tell you that any investment that gives more than a 4 percent return is high yield and based on mortgage interest rates for a fifteen-year adjustable-rate at around 2 percent (at the time of this writing). I can see why they tell clients that. When I started investing in high yields, it wasn't hard to get 15 percent or more as an average ROI (return on investment). If I have a holding with an ROI that dropped to

8 percent, I would sell it because I can always get a better ROI with another stock. That is why stocks are still my investment of choice, and I still get at least 15 percent average return on my stock investments.

Another very popular investment that pays you money back is rental properties. Many, many people have chosen this venue to earn a monthly income, and this is a safe, tried-and-true way to earn return on investment. Unlike stocks, real estate is tangible and easy to see, touch, and feel. I own real estate, but it is not for investment income.

My property first and foremost fills my business needs and generates a small amount of rental income. The equity of that property has allowed me to tap into funds for investment. What doesn't appeal to me about rental property is the unannounced demand on my time, such as a late-night call from a tenant telling you the hot water tank just sprung a leak.

Stocks never call you at night. In fact, they never call. Real estate is a great way to get money from your investments. Millions of people have done it, thousands of books have been written about it, and it will still be a great way to get money in the future. I do not like to be beholden to a tenant and on call twenty-four hours a day. Stocks are beholden to me. If I don't like what they are doing, I get rid of them with the click of a button.

I don't even need a stockbroker as my father did early on in his investment journey. If I fall out of love with my rental property and want to get rid of it, I have to comply with someone or an agency, which requires me to take my time and money to make requested and/or required repairs. On top of that, the property will have to be listed with a real estate agent who gets a percentage of the initial investment return. Sell it yourself takes up your free time, and even if you do sell it yourself, you still need an attorney to make sure there aren't any problems with the sale, but even that is no guarantee a problem won't haunt you.

7

Stocks Are the Greatest And Easiest Way To Get An Extra Paycheck

Now that you have opened a brokerage account and have money to put into buying stocks, how do you maximize the laws of compound interest to work for you? Fund this account with as much money as you possibly can, making sure that you will not need any of the money for an emergency. This is not the place to put emergency funds or any funds that you might need for short-term use. Use money that you will not need to get your hands on for at least six months.

This brokerage account should be used to generate an income stream, but as it grows, you will see how much more flexible and useful this account will become. My favorite way to describe this account is it can become your goose-that-lays-the-golden-eggs account, depending on how much your start with. Initially, it will start generating monthly and quarterly dividends that, when reinvested, will start compounding the money you previously earned the very next month. You will now be earning interest on your interest.

Example

$10,000.00 Invested @ 15% interest = $125.00 per month

$10,125.00 @ 15% int. = $126.56 per mo

$10,251.56 @ 15% int. = $128.14 per mo

$10,379.70 @ 15% int. = $129.75 per mo

$10,509.45 @ 15% int. = $131.37 per mo

$10,640.82 @ 15% int. = $133.01 per mo

$10,773.83 @ 15% int. = $134.67 per mo

$10,908.50 @ 15% int. = $136.37 per mo

$11,044.86 @ 15% int. = $138.06 per mo.

$11,182.92 @ 15% int. = $139.79 per mo.

$11,322.71 @ 15% int. = $141.53 per mo.

$11,464.24 @ 15% int. = $143.30 per mo.

By reinvesting the dividends monthly, you gain an extra $107.54 for twelve months as opposed to a straight 15 percent on $10,000, which would be $1,500 versus $1,607.54, netting the difference of $107.54.

You might notice the similarity between my example and a typical passbook savings from any bank in the country. The monthly interest is paid on the balance every month. The compound interest also applies here. Even when banks have paid enough interest on savings, stocks pay more.

A few operational issues need to be mentioned when you make a purchase in your brokerage account. There will be a fee for your purchase, which range from around $4.95 to $12, depending upon who you sign up with. These fees have dropped substantially since I first started trading. Trading fees were $29 per trade from discount brokerage firms.

Banks do not charge you to deposit money like a brokerage account does for your investment transactions. In the scope of this plan, it really is a nonissue. A dividend reinvestment plan (DRP) is a way around these fees in your brokerage account. Your dividends will automatically be reinvested with the stock that is paying the dividend—at no charge. The only thing you have to do is get online and watch it grow. You will certainly want to take advantage of this when the dividends you receive each month are not very large, such as in the previous example.

Once your monthly dividend reaches $1,500 or $2,000, you will want to direct those dividends to your holdings that may be down in price to take advantage of garage-sale prices. This sometimes helps give your investments a little bit more horsepower for your ROI every month. Not every stock will allow you to do this. You have to check for this service at the time of purchase.

You may switch from automatic reinvestment to cash—and back again—pretty much at will. When starting with investing in high-yield stocks, the key is put that dividend money back into the investment as quickly as possible. The DRP is the best way to do that.

Don't buy high-yield stocks that won't let you DRP until you have enough funds to self-direct with a larger amount of money. I own a couple of high-yield stocks that won't allow DRP, but I get enough of a dividend from them that reinvestment each month doesn't always include me purchasing that stock. I will purchase what is paying the best or what has gone down in value but pays the same dividend rate.

8

How To Take Advantage Of
A Wall Street Yard Sale

The main reason for getting and keeping the compound
interest machine going was best demonstrated with the bowl

of rice example since compound interest starts out small and somewhat insignificant. However, if you stick to this plan by reinvesting the dividends and adding new money to increase the amount of dividends you get each month, you will have even better results than simple compound interest.

By reinvesting the dividends and adding new money, you are accelerating the laws of compound interest. A few things can help you maximize your efforts. Almost all of your holdings will pay dividends to your account on the first of the month, but some will pay by the tenth of the month. This money will show up in your account as cash. You can do anything you want with this cash. However, if you want to get your money back into the system, you only have a few days to do so. When you look at the stock data you are buying, you will see the ex-dividend date. You must make your stock purchase before that date in order to get the additional dividend on the stock you are buying by the first of the next month. An ex-dividend date of February 10, 2016, means you must own the stock by end of market closing on February 9, 2016, to get your dividend on March 1, 2016. Any break in the cycle of reinvesting your dividends stops your compound cycle. The price of the stock determines the worth of your stock when you buy and sell it, but it is not a clear indication of the stock's value.

I buy stocks for their ability to pay me cash every month. Although the price of the stock has my attention, it is not the determining factor for buying or selling it. The stocks I own are my geese that lay golden eggs. I have owned some stocks for more than twenty years—through up and down markets. The only reason I have held onto them is because of their ability to provide a large return every month on time, without fail.

When the stock market tumbled in 2008, everyone lost worth on the price of their stocks. All of my stocks were down at least 30 percent.

My mother-in law said, "You don't seem to be upset about the stock market downturn. Why?"

I wasn't upset at all. I didn't like seeing the numbers of my account being so low, but I knew it was a cycle and that things would eventually come back up. If you don't get anything else out of this book, please get this: my dividend-paying stocks provide the same dividends throughout this down market as they did when the market was normal, even, and calm.

A downturn in stock prices creates a Wall Street yard sale for the buy-and-hold investor. This is a great opportunity to buy more stocks that pay you to own them. On top of getting your dividends back in, it is a great opportunity to throw more money at the stocks that are offered at bargain-basement prices.

You must fight conventional thinking, which scares people away from investing in the stock market. Many people who don't fully understand the inherent nature of the market will sell in a panic, lose money, and profess how risky it is to be in the stock market. This is not to say that I don't sell my stocks—I do—but it is not for conventional reasons.

When I purchase a stock, it is because all the criteria has been met for that stock to provide me with a monthly or quarterly stream of cash. My goal for purchasing a stock is that it will contribute to my total goal of 15 percent total ROI annually. That stock needs to be paying between 12 percent and 22 percent. If I buy a stock that pays a 15 percent dividend annually, and the cost of the stock is $10 per share, its dividend will be .12½ cents per share every month. Over twelve months, that equals $1.50 per share annually. If I own 1,000 shares of that stock, in twelve months, that stock will have paid me $1,500 or $125 per month. My initial investment is $10,000.

Let's apply my rule of 72 to another example: 72 ÷ 15 = 4.8. It will take 4.8 years for $10,000 to double to $20,000. That is a pretty good way to make money. Now that the stock has grown to $20 per share and is still paying 12½ cents per share, I get $1,500 a year since I still own 1,000 shares. I still get $125 per month.

The stock holdings I bought for $10,000 (1,000 shares @ $10 each = $10,000) are now worth $20,000 (1,000 shares @ $20 each = $20,000). It has doubled in value. Conventional thinking would say, "Wow! I need to buy more of that!" Wrong! In fact, it is a stock that I want to sell!

My initial investment of $10,000 was paying 15 percent ROI ($1,500 per year). The last example shows that this stock doubled in price, netting a $10,000 gain and doubling my investment worth, but the dividends (ROI) dropped to half of what it was paying. The dividend is now paying 7.5 percent instead of 15 percent, which was my model standard.

By selling this stock, I have new cash to reinvest ($20,000) plus all the money I have collected along the way to this stock doubling in price. This is even a better compounding scenario than reinvesting your dividends every month because of its growth in price. This doesn't happen often, but it does happen.

At the time of this writing, I happened upon an energy stock that was on the edge of acceptability. It was paying about 11 percent, which is still very high by industry standards. What caught my eye about this stock other than its high yield was the fact that it had a very stable chart—for a long period of time. At the time I was looking to buy it, most energy and oil companies' prices were low due to the abundance of oil on hand worldwide.

Oil from fracking was stored and ready for processing, but what kept this company so steady? After digging into it, I found that they were into all types of energy and not just oil. They were into solar power, wind power, hydrokinetics, and other forms of energy. It was a no-brainer, and it fit all my criteria. This stock paid quarterly. After two quarters, the stock started to rise in price after news came out that there was an offer to buy this company by another company with a similar profile that was in multiple forms of energy.

After looking at the buying company, I discovered their stock offering was higher in price and paid a lower dividend (6 percent). I would never give this company a second look on my quest for "fresh meat." I thought, *If this company does buy the one I'm holding, the dividends will go the way of buying company. I will sell out, which is not what I like to do. I like to buy and hold like Warren Buffett.*

The purchase did happen, and the dividends did drop. The price of the stock is rising, and I will be selling my holdings within months—if not sooner. It has doubled in price and will ultimately contribute to the compound interest program that is my model. This demonstrates another mathematic principle that is a key element for the high-yield investment model. Once you have purchased a stock that has a set dividend, watch what the price of the stock does to the percentage of the dividend in relation to the rate of return. When a stock climbs in price, the percentage of the dividend in relation to the ROI goes down. This rule is based on the dividend paying the same amount per share. This indicator is a great snapshot to let you know if it is time to sell or buy more.

Let's use the price of the previous example to illustrate this point. The stock price is $10 per share and pays a dividend of 15 percent, which equals $1.50 per share per year, which equals 12.5 cents per month per share. If the stock grows to $20 per share, and the dividend pays exactly the same $1.50 per share per year (12.5 cents per month per share), the percentage of the dividend in relation to the price of the stock drops from its initial price percentage from 15 percent to 7.5 percent. You are not earning as high a percentage on your investment if you buy it at $20 per share. The stock in this example at $20 per share would not fit into my model; therefore, I would not buy it. However, I would buy this stock at $10 per share, and I even may hold onto it until it reaches $20 per share. If that happens very quickly (within a year), I would sell. If it takes several years, I'd be in no rush to sell unless I needed the gain in price for a better-paying investment.

The goal here is to get a flock of geese laying golden eggs with larger and more eggs coming your way every month that you faithfully put back to work compounding your interest. You soon will have enough every month to help grow your wealth in other ways. With this cash-generating system in place and running smoothly, you will reach a point where your monthly income matches what you are bringing home. That is your extra paycheck, which you can put back into your compounding machine or use to help with expenses.

My favorite way is to fund your retirement account with the dividends. This is a separate account, which financial planners call "qualified money." This is a great way to keep the compound interest machine going because you can use the same investment for your retirement account.

My next favorite way to generate wealth with your dividends is to use those dividends to pay a fixed monthly bill that comes out of your monthly expenses. For most people, that will be their mortgage. Once you have built up your monthly cash flow to the point where it is close to being an extra paycheck, you should be able to let your dividends help you out with some larger debts. Generally speaking, the home mortgage takes the biggest bite out of most people's budget. Wouldn't it be great if you could get that monthly payment handled by other means than your take-home pay? If you can contribute monthly to an investment plan, you can take advantage of buying dates and stick to them. You will see the cash grow because the stocks are paying you for your investment efforts.

Let me illustrate an example of additional wealth building. You have a monthly income from your stock dividends of $1,000 per month, but instead of reinvesting it in a compound interest earning machine, you would like to use some of that monthly income to pay your mortgage. Great idea! I would set it up to happen effortlessly.

If your mortgage is $500 per month—and your brokerage account is generating $1,000 per month—I would leave those dividends in cash for two monthly cycles ($2,000). I would tell your mortgage lender to have the mortgage payment taken directly out of your brokerage account the very next month, which would be the third monthly cycle.

After the third cycle, you will have $3,000. After your mortgage payment is deducted, you will have $2,500 in cash. When you reinvest your dividend money in the compound interest machine, it will only be $500 because your mortgage is being paid by your monthly dividends. Your home is being paid off with free money that did not come out of your take-home pay. You cut your reinvestment money in half, which affects the rate of growth, but you have more of your take-home pay.

After your mortgage has been paid for a couple of cycles, part of the extra money that has been sitting as cash in your brokerage account ($2,500) should be put back into the reinvestment cycle—but only after you are sure the direct payment for your mortgage is working smoothly. The $2,500 in cash is doing nothing. Leave two mortgage payments in reserve, which will be $1,000, and then put the $1,500 back to work.

It will not take long if you keep the momentum going. You'll soon be back to the $1,000 monthly dividend—and your house will be automatically paid for every month. Having a major debt being paid for every month will become so comfortable and effortless that when you get a statement at the end of the year, you will be shocked to see the lower balance owed because the payments are automatic. You won't notice them; it will be like they don't exist.

This plan will take a lot of hard work and sacrifice, but once you have tasted the freedom of managing your debt and systematically building your wealth, you will never accept anything less. This process and these steps can be repeated time and time again without fail as long as the stock continues to pay a dividend!

You might ask, "Why should I go through the trouble of paying my mortgage out of my brokerage account? Why not just have it taken out of my household checking account?"

The money you get in that paycheck has all the taxes taken out before you get it. That is why it is so small compared to what it should be. Depending on your income, it can be anywhere between 15 percent and 35 percent. It is shameful that we give up that much of our earnings.

Early in my career, I checked to see how much I was paying in taxes on money earned, property taxes, use tax (mostly gasoline), sales tax, and hospitality tax. I was paying 52 percent of my gross pay in some type of tax. It probably would not hurt so much if we got the maximum for what we contribute, but I think most people agree that we don't get the full services we pay for. If you pay your mortgage out of your paycheck, you're paying with after-tax dollars, which is taking a bigger bite out of your money. When you pay for your mortgage out of your brokerage account, you will be paying with money that has not been taxed yet. When you are taxed for that money, you will be ahead of the tax burden because that money is taxed at a lower rate. It is taxed as unearned income, and everything that comes out of your paycheck is taxed at an earned-income rate.

Unearned income is taxed at a 15 percent rate, which should be about half of your earned income tax rate. This is an advantage to you because Uncle Sam is not getting his hands on your money before you do. You will not pay tax on that money for more than a year. You are compounding interest for 15½ months before the taxes are due on its growth. Also, you will be able to deduct the interest you're paying the lender that is carrying your mortgage, which lessens your tax liability.

To cover my tax liabilities, I hold back the money I will need to pay my tax liabilities to Uncle Sam and the state income tax between December and April 15. This takes a little bit of forecasting, but it is generally pretty close. I am not paying taxes with money that has already been taxed. On top of that, I'm paying the debt with money that won't be taxed until the next tax year.

If you are making a lot of extra money, Uncle Sam wants you to send estimated tax payments. I always get into arguments with my accountant about this. I would prefer to not send in the estimated tax money, keep it, earn the interest, and pay the penalty for lack of estimated payments. I would prefer not to give Uncle Sam ten cents more than I have to—any sooner than I have to.

For the record, I don't recommend doing this. It is just a pet peeve of mine. These examples that I have shown are ways that demonstrate a safe and simple way to build wealth automatically by compounding interest to snowball into a large cache of money that helps pay everyday expenses while still growing. Money is the sharpest, most versatile, and most useful tool. We all need tools to do good work. If you buy good tools and learn how to use them properly, I promise, you will do great work.

9

Other Sources Of Free Money

There are many other ways to get money that you can use to put into your compound interest machine. I use one of the most evil demons that plague our society through its mishandling. It is the greatest enabler to spending money that you don't have—with no pain until the bill comes. This demon is credit cards.

I have read so many books that on my quest for financial independence, and they all mention the evils of credit cards. Several books suggest cutting them up or never having them. Others equate them to giving heroin to a heroin addict. If you can't control your spending, you should not be using credit cards. If that is the case, you are in need of professional help—and my tips won't be of any use to you anyway. You cannot travel, rent a car, or book a hotel without a credit card. I travel for my business to the tune of 100,000 miles per year in addition to my vacation travel. It would not be easy—and maybe even impossible—to do that without credit cards.

I have a quick little horror story about not having a credit card. Late in his life, my father went to visit his old air force buddies who he hadn't seen for more than fifty years. He didn't have a credit card, but he bought tickets and lodging through a travel agent. I had his itinerary and was waiting at the gate for his return flight. I watched every last person get off that plane—but no Thomas. I thought he missed his flight.

He finally called me to inform me that he didn't realize the date of his return flight and had missed it completely. He had to stay out west one more day and book a new ticket to get my mother and him home, but he didn't have enough cash with him to pay for it all. He borrowed it from a friend so he could get home. Foolish! When he got back, we got him a credit card that he used for everything he could.

To get money by using your credit cards, you must pay off your balance every month—without exception. If you cannot or will not pay off the balance every month, don't bother reading this chapter. Not having a credit card will cripple your mobility. If you must have one to function, why not get one that will help you get money?

Many credit cards pay rewards that include 2 percent back, free air miles, or free gas. Take a little time to find one that suits your needs before signing up. Keep it simple and go for the cash. Getting 2 percent back for buying things you need anyway is another source of free money.

Most card statements will show how much cash that you have racked up each month. That's like having your own little savings account. I like to wait for the money to grow to a certain point before taking it out or using it for something I would like to buy for myself that I wouldn't ordinarily use my everyday budget for. I will charge my purchase and then redeem my rewards to cover the cost of the item. Several years ago, I learned to ski with my son. It was something we both loved and enjoyed together. I was getting pretty good at it, but I was tired of using rentals.

After finding the skis I wanted, at my price point, I charged the skis to my charge card. I used the rewards to cover the cost. It felt like my rich uncle had just sent me a great present.

Over the years, I have redeemed thousands of dollars for my brokerage account and used it to invest or treat myself to purchases. Those reward dollars are your money, and it comes out of the money you pay on your monthly charges. You will not get a 1099 tax form from the credit card company because it is really your money. It is great marketing on the part of the credit card companies!

My business has a rewards credit card, and all of our employees use the card to make purchases on behalf of the office. We even trust contract help to carry the cards. We get the benefits of the payback rewards, and we get an itemized statement of all expenditures categorized according to the job.

Another major use of our rewards card was developed by my wife. When we have wholesale vendors that take payment with credit cards and our purchases are larger than our card limit, she will charge her order to the card's limit, and then write a check to the credit card company right away. When the account gets cleared, she goes back and charges the balance of the order. It's a little bit of work for 2 percent return. This practice has netted thousands of dollars that would have been otherwise lost or not even realized. It's free money because you're making the purchase regardless of the reward or not.

Another little trick that my wife has capitalized on is the

local grocery store fuel perks. This is where our local grocery stores give you free gasoline based on the amount of money you spend with them. She will buy the store gift cards along with gift cards for restaurants and various other stores where she has to make purchases. Then, she charges all those gift cards with her 2 percent rewards credit card. She gets 2 percent back on her purchases, and she gets free gasoline for buying the gift cards at the local grocery store. We have figured out that she gets enough free gas for her car for almost an entire year.

This can be a serious amount of money over a year, especially if you have to make the purchase anyway. Why not get the money that is available to you for the taking? There is also another very common everyday way to get money: coupons. Coupons can be very valuable in the form of price discounts or free products. Either way, it can be less money out of your pocket for things you are going to buy or have to buy.

Many people have made a living clipping coupons or made lots of money printing counterfeit coupons. Coupons are real money and can be used daily in almost all areas of consuming goods and services. My wife and I both went through failed marriages with little money. We managed to have a great time doing things together that coupons afforded us the opportunity to do so. We could go to see exhibits at museums with two-for-one coupons and get two-for-one dinners at decent restaurants—among many other events and places. To this day, even though we are in a much better financial situation, we still make an effort to use coupons that are available to us.

The extra little savings we get is not embarrassing or degrading as some people might think. We feel that it is completely the opposite; it is being a good steward of our blessings. If you want to get even a little more out of your savings with coupons, set the savings you get from coupons aside as cash. Every three to six months, put that money into your brokerage account to invest. In a year, you will have more money compounding interest for you.

If you track the savings, you will see how little efforts add up to substantial amounts of money over the years. I don't track my savings with coupons or fuel perks, but I have studied the efforts and know the results. I do it automatically. Tracking your savings can show you how much you can save without cutting into your budget.

10

Borrowing To Invest?!...Don't Be Stupid

This is definitely the most contrarian section of this book. Unless you have adopted my model for compounding interest, this chapter will be nothing but poppycock and very risky to implement. I have always hated being in debt or owing somebody money. It feels a little unsettling in my stomach. The bottom line is that debt is bad. Make no mistake. However, using credit cards to gain dollars is a perfect exercise in asset management.

Consumer debt is evil and a lust for things, which is not at all what we are talking about. Every financial management book I have read describes consumer debt as destructive and something to be avoided. A famous financial advisor says that no debt is good—and it should be avoided at all cost. I am certain that he is talking about personal debt. I think that type of thinking is extreme and radical. If you can borrow without being in harm's way and profit from it, that is being a good steward with your assets.

A small business owner who relies on clients to pay on

time is subject to cash flow crunches. Money does not always come in on time or exactly when it is needed. You might get a payment from a client that was larger than you thought it would be. That money can put you ahead a little—until the bill from the IRS says you didn't pay them enough on your taxes two years ago. There may be tax, interest, and penalties. Does that sound familiar?

It is important to have a good credit history. Being able to borrow at a moment's notice is crucial for keeping your business moving forward. I have used my line of credit with the bank that handles my company's checking account. My line of credit can be funded with a phone call. Assets can be added to the company checking account, and monthly payments can be automatically deducted from the company's checking account.

This arrangement is renewed annually with an administrative fee and a rate of interest for the year. Since I have payments deducted automatically, my credit with our bank is always in great standing. After doing this a couple of times, I saw that I had access to a fairly large amount of money for a little bit of interest for one year—as many times as needed that year. Why not take that money for the full year, invest it, let the dividends pay the monthly payment, and keep the difference, thus starting a company savings account? It was a great way to create a savings account for my business. It was a type of forced savings. It was also a great way for me to borrow money at a low rate and make more money than I was paying on the borrowed amount. This is how it worked out→

Example

Borrowing your way to riches

	Principle	Payment	Interest
January	$10,000.00	$833.00	$33.33
February	$9,167.00	$833.00	$30.56
March	$8,334.00	$833.00	$27.78
April	$7,501.00	$833.00	$25.00
May	$6,668.00	$833.00	$22.23
June	$5,835.00	$833.00	$19.45
July	$5,002.00	$833.00	$16.67
August	$4,169.00	$833.00	$13.90
September	$3,336.00	$833.00	$11.12
October	$2,503.00	$833.00	$8.34
November	$1,607.00	$833.00	$5.57
December	$837.00	$837.00	$2.79

TOTAL COST OF LOAN $10,000 + $216.74 = $10,216.74

EARNINGS ON $10,000 @15% DIVIDEND

$10,000 + $1,500 = $11,500 - $10,216.74

PROFIT FROM LOAN $1,283.26

I told my accountant that I was going to borrow on my line of credit to start a company savings account, and I told him how I was going to do it.

He said, "I didn't know you were that much of a gambler."

I said, "I'm not. In fact, I hate gambling. How is this any different from borrowing money for rental properties that generate income?"

He said, "Okay. I'll buy that. If you have the money, why not just put the money in savings?"

The only reason for not doing that is cash flow. I did not want to disturb any of my working capital. One of the largest points of misunderstanding is that investing in stocks is very dangerous. I don't think you will find any financial advisor or planner who will advocate borrowing money to invest in the stock market.

I have read many books that advocate buying investment property with no money down and not using your own money. I see danger in that kind of thinking. Taking on a large debt, such as a house that cannot be liquidated quickly and is a huge risk, leaves me with body parts exposed, and I'm not willing to have them uncovered. If something goes south and you need cash right away, you're stuck! This is not to say that real estate is not a good investment—it most certainly is. I have real estate investments that provide me a positive cash flow.

Stocks can be liquidated on a moment's notice. Selling real estate is like turning an ocean liner, and selling stocks is like turning a jet ski. There are many, many horror stories of people losing everything in the stock market. They are absolutely true. This reputation that the stock market has of being a huge gamble is also very true, but the majority of the risk can be taken out with a little effort researching the golden nuggets that are there for the taking.

Borrowing for investment is just as good and no riskier than owning rental property—only with a lot fewer headaches. You can borrow to invest in the stock market, but don't be stupid. I have several loans, and every loan is generating some form of income. I have no consumer loans. That is not to say that I won't take out a loan if I want to buy a new car. I will. However, I will pay that loan off with investment earnings and not money from my paycheck.

Before I take on any debt, I evaluate whether I can get rid of it with a minimum of pain if something goes wrong. I have absolutely no debt that cannot be satisfied if needed and not change my family's life style. I will not take risks that could put me in harm's way. This model for borrowing bucks conventional reasoning and is totally contrarian to mainstream financial planning. Don't be stupid. I don't suggest investing like this until you have a well-oiled, time-tested, proven investment model that you can operate and maintain effortlessly.

For those of you who like real estate as an investment, here is my story. In 2006, I was driving down a main road in my town. Not far from downtown, I noticed a for sale sign on a property that I was very familiar with. I was stunned to see it was the oldest farmhouse in our city, and it was fairly well preserved. I quickly turned into the driveway and got the phone number of the listing agent. My wife was working in a real estate office, and I asked her to give me the number of their commercial agent. I told her I would explain later.

I had first noticed the house when I was eighteen years old. I was working for a contractor on a property just two doors down. When I noticed the property for the first time, with its very striking barn stone structure, I thought, *How cool is that house? I wonder what the inside looks like.*

Several years later, I was sent to the house to pick up some drawings for my boss. I went to the front door and thought, *Someday I'm going to buy this place.*

I can see it as clearly as if it happened yesterday. Thirty years later, I did just that. Coincidence? I think not. Divine guidance attracted me to the building.

I called the commercial agent from my wife's office and went to see the property the very next day.

When we walked in the door, a feeling or a sensation filled my body. I did not need to see the rest of this property. I knew it was going to be mine. After touring the house and finding out what they were asking for, my conviction about buying the property was reinforced.

Then the listing agent said, "Let's go look at the barn. There is some really interesting space in there."

Unknown to me, there was a second building tucked away on the property. It was hidden by some trees. I could not believe my eyes. It was way beyond my expectations. After seeing the second building and finding out they were both included for the same price, I couldn't get out of there fast enough. *I am buying this building. It is more than anything I ever imagined.*

We got in the car after thanking everybody for their time.

The door wasn't even latched when I said, "I'm buying this place."

My wife said, "Whoa, cowboy. You might want to think about this."

I said to our agent, "Let's go somewhere to write an offer."

After dinner—and very little reasoning things out—we came up with a plan and an offer. I wanted one other person to see this house before I pulled the trigger, and that was my accountant. He was my friend who had to liquidate fifty-nine rental properties in his brother's estate, and he did not like property very much as an investment or otherwise. He preferred the freedom and flexibility of renting. Even though I was prepared for a negative review, I still wanted him to see it.

We met him at the property with an offer in hand, gave him a quick rundown of my thoughts, and showed him the outline of my offer.

He said, "Okay. Let's take a look."

We took one step inside, closed the door, and I turned around.

He whispered over my shoulder, "Buy it."

For the second time in as many visits, I was filled with the energy and spirit that lived in the house. I knew right then and there that it was going to happen. Everything was falling into place.

The process moved quickly. My friend Ky arranged a loan, and as we signed papers for the largest loan I had ever committed to, I felt complete peace about the property, the debt, and the future. I was not just the owner. I was the caretaker.

When I looked back at the chain of events that led me to buying a historical landmark that needed a lot of repair, it became very clear that I was a part of a much bigger plan, a larger responsibility, and a larger mission. It was apparent by the spirit inside of me and the energy I felt the minute I walked in the door that God wanted me to take over the care and restoration of the property. That house would become my office.

Little coincidences are really building blocks that carve out how and why. After the loan was secured, I told my accountant that I wanted to vanquish that fifteen-year loan sooner than the full term. I would have to apply additional money to the loan each month. My loan was a commercial loan, and even though it was originally a private home, it had been rezoned to commercial many years before my purchase.

Commercial loans at the time of purchase required a minimum 20 percent down payment. When I made an offer to buy the farmhouse, we had just finished a fourteen-unit contract, and my final payment for the prior two years of work was finally in the bank. The amount required for my end of the purchase—the 20 percent required by the bank—was *exactly* the amount I had in my company's savings account. Another coincidence? I think not!

With the increased debt and the need to make all my payments, I needed an increase in revenue to keep my head above water. The first thing I did was incorporate the farmhouse. That way, my business could rent space from the farmhouse corporation. The farmhouse came with a paying tenant, which helped a lot with the monthly expenses.

The first few months are the toughest for getting settled into debts. Once it all got settled, it leveled out. However, I still needed more revenue to cover the expenses and repairs. As my needs grew, so did my blessings. My business grew, and we added more staff. Even more contracts came in, and I was able to make extra payments to the loan and make more repairs. My fifteen-year note was vanquished in eleven years almost to the month that Ky professed to the bank that I would have the debt paid off.

Ky never got to celebrate the mortgage burning with me. He passed away, leaving a huge void in me. I knew nothing about business financing and related taxes before him. He would have been proud of my accomplishment in making his word to the bank golden.

Even though there was no longer a mortgage on the farmhouse, the structural repairs required even more money than the cosmetic ones. The only way I could figure out how to manage that task was with another loan. A second mortgage meant more debt. I had all this capital sitting in the farmhouse and doing nothing for my cause.

It dawned on me that my need for cash to do the repairs

was no different than my mother's need for cash when she was in hospice. The difference was that I had no large cache to generate an income stream. I could have one if I borrowed against the value of the farmhouse. That was not a brilliant revelation; many people take equity out of their homes to do other things with the money that has accrued. Developers continue building on the value of their properties. This practice is common today, but using high-yield stocks to create an income stream by borrowing the money is considered as solid as nailing Jell-O to a tree.

The more I thought about it, the more it made sense to me. I had been doing it successfully for almost twenty years. The biggest difference was that I would be doing it with borrowed money. I liked the idea a lot. It solved my needs, and I knew how to make it work.

Greg was my new accountant, a financial advisor, and a trusted friend. When we first met and agreed on our business arrangement, he began looking over my company's finances. After reviewing everything, he said, "I noticed you have a company brokerage account. What is that all about?"

I told him what I had been doing with high-yield stocks and how I was trying to build savings for my company so that I could protect the company from slow-paying clients or a downturn in business.

He understood the savings part, but he questioned the investment in the stock market as a safe, secure place for emergency money. I told him that I was averaging a 15 percent return.

He looked at me like a deer in the headlights and said, "You need to show me this."

It took him less than a minute to look over the numbers. "Wow. Okay. I get it."

After several meetings, we worked out a larger picture for growth on all fronts, including my idea to remortgage the farmhouse and create an income stream for the major repairs that need to be done. He gave me his blessing and said that my plan and my investment model were truly sound fiscal thinking. He added that borrowing money to invest in the stock market was extremely unconventional and that most people would not get it. I am making my mortgage money work even harder, and it is helping me gain more wealth. It is similar to the example of the other paycheck. The difference is that we need to have more safeguards in place because it is borrowed money.

Extra care should be taken in setting up a mortgage payback model. You need to establish the amount of money you will receive in the form of a check or direct deposit. Since there will be bank charges attached to the loan, make sure you take them into account when figuring out your net amount to be received. You need to establish the payment you will be committed to every month. You need to come up with the monthly loan payback amount and automatically deduct it from your account. When calculating the monthly payback amount, add a minimum of $50 to the loan principal. This shortens your debit duration by several months, strengthens your credit score because the payment is always on time, and builds trust between you and your lender.

Here are how the numbers work out for this loan example: Borrow $100,000 at 4.75 percent interest, and the duration of the loan is fifteen years. The monthly loan payment is $825 principal and interest plus $50 additional principal payment, making the monthly payment $875 ($10,500 annually). From the investment side, $100,000 invested in high-yield stocks nets 15 percent dividends annually, which is $15,000 ($1,250 per month).

- Monthly income from investment of $1,250
- Less mortgage payment interest, principal, and additional principal ($875) = $375
- $375 x 12 = $4,500 annual earnings after loan payment

This self-sustaining loan gives me an extra $4,500 per year to apply to savings, repairs, or whatever else is needed. It isn't all that much, but this loan is paying for itself—along with a $375 per month bonus. This is a boost to my positive cash flow, which is generated by the other rental income. Now I have plenty of income to make repairs.

With the second additional income stream from the loan investment and the rental income, the next step is to create an additional safeguard and put it into place. This income stream has a debt attached to it; therefore, I want emergency money within this model. I hold one year's worth of mortgage payments in cash so that if something should go dreadfully wrong, I can hold the bank off for one full year, which would give me plenty of time to liquidate assets and vanquish all debt—and do it in a calm state and not a panic.

I am holding almost $11,000 in cash, which is not working for me, but that same thinking kept my father almost 100 percent invested in the market. A small amount of money held in reserve is an insurance policy that I don't have to pay for; in fact, it is actually free money. This reserve money also gives me the freedom to budget and schedule repairs without the fear of running out of cash. I set aside extra cash twice a year so that property taxes aren't as much of a burden as they have been in the past, and I am paying them off with free money.

These loan models have worked, and they are working for me today. They provide greater flexibility that only the greatest tool in your toolbox can provide: cash. This model for borrowing is absolutely no different than borrowing money to buy an apartment building that is full of renters that provide a positive cash flow every month. The difference is that stocks don't get a leaky roof or move out, which can lower your cash flow.

The greatest advantage to borrowing this way and having a safeguard of cash is the ability to get out of debt on a moment's notice. Sell the stocks, pay back the loan, and experience freedom.

If you have to liquidate the stocks and get out of the investments, you could be "upside-down" on your investments (which means you would get less for the investment than what you owe). If you monitor the movement of the stocks and keep track of your earnings, that should never be the case. Over time, your principal should always be greater than the loan balance. That is how your loan is providing you wealth. If you practice this model over time, depending on your financial goals, you can create total independence through borrowing— just don't be stupid.

PART 3

Mortgages: The American Dream

11

Own Your Own Home, It Is An Investment... Maybe, Maybe Not

I grew up in the fifties in a *Leave It to Beaver* neighborhood. The postwar era created a Pollyanna atmosphere for our family of four. We had a cute little house with a used car and a garage (my father never owned a brand-new car and thought cars were "bad investments"). I had a stay-at-home mom, and the kids walked to school. It was much harder for my parents to make ends meet than we saw on television. Our neighborhood was clean, safe, and full of working-class rubber workers. It was a snapshot of an American neighborhood, and all of our neighbors had mortgages on their houses.

I was born the day my parents moved into our house. They had a mortgage rate of 4 percent on a house that had a selling price of $8,000. That was average for pretty much every house in our school district. The people living in those homes were living out the American dream.

What is the American dream today? I'm not sure I would know how to describe it, but owning a home is still part of most family's lives. Owning a home has given me a wide variety of experiences and a wide variety of financing solutions. When you have to shop for a mortgage, use these nuggets of advice to create rewarding results.

Land Contract

My first house was an impulse purchase that I made with my college roommate. In the late seventies, the housing market was good. A lot of people were buying older houses—fixer-uppers—and flipping them. We had friends who were doing it and making good money.

My roommate was always looking to make some extra money, and he was always looking for a deal. He approached me with a "great deal" he had found. Surprisingly enough, it was on the outer edge of the North Hill section where I grew up. This neighborhood was rougher, but it still had a lot of older Polish and Italian immigrants as steadfast residents.

When we went to look at the house Butch had found, we were able to go right in through a broken window off the front porch. The vacant two-story Dutch colonial house was typical for that area. It had been built in the early 1900s, and it had a beautiful staircase and woodwork. Butch told me the house was $8,500, but the owner would sell it on a land contract, which meant he would carry the papers. We just had to pay him monthly plus 4 percent interest annually.

Our monthly payment was $150 with a balloon payment at the end of four years. At the end of the four years, the balance of our loan was due (less our four years of payments):

150 x 48 = $7,200
$8,500 - $7,200 = $1,300

We both laughed! We thought we would have that thing flipped in four months.

I was in my last year of college, and I thought it wouldn't take up that much time to flip it with both of us working on it. We had done a few remodeling projects together, and we had a feel for working with each other. A couple of good friends working on a project to make a few bucks didn't seem risky.

We signed the papers with the owner (without the counsel of an attorney—stupid), got the keys, and things went sour. Butch ducked out on me. He got cold feet, and he was in a much better position to handle it than I was.

I started to panic. Now what? My conscience wouldn't let me walk away before I got in too deep. My parents raised us to stand by our commitments, and integrity was important to them.

I was working hard to finish my last year of college. I was working full-time to pay for my education, and I wasn't sure how I was going to manage my commitments. After much vacillating, I decided to move into the disheveled house. That was probably the only way I would be able to do any work on it with motivation—by being stuck in the middle of it. I had the utilities turned on (water, electric, and gas), which was a little bit of a problem since that the previous renter had skipped out on the final payments. It was less than twenty-five bucks for water and electric, but when I tried to get the gas turned on, a $400 charge put the brakes on things.

I moved my meager possessions into an upstairs bedroom with no heat and no hope of getting it turned on anytime soon. I felt trapped. In order to keep the house from being vandalized, the neighbors needed to see someone living in the house. In early March, the nights were very cold—and there was still the occasional snowfall. Even though it was sunny and warm outside, it was an icebox inside.

I would tough it out by living there with no heat until I could scrape up enough money to get the gas turned on. I kept my food, limited as it was, in a garbage bag and hung it outside the upstairs window to keep the perishables from spoiling. I was camping out in my own house—well, almost my own house.

After about three weeks of my arctic excursion, I came up with enough money to get the gas turned on. It was so pleasant to have heat and hot water that I didn't even notice how much work needed to be done to make the place livable. When my first gas bill came after only about ten days, the bill showed that I had used $35 in gas and that I had a credit on account of $365. Seeing that huge credit of money sent me to the moon.

After several calls, I got a refund check. Once everything was straightened out, it was just a matter of fixing up the place so I could sell it. By the end of that summer, a strange thing happened: I fell in love with that house.

Things were starting to take shape. The repairs brought to light the hidden treasures that the house was hiding in its disrepair. The payments were manageable, and because I was doing my own work, I could afford to put a little nicer finishing touches into my home. The land contract purchase ended up being a boon to launching my financial journey. It took less than two years to pay off the owner. I put about another $20,000 into materials to improve it, and I ended up living there for eight more years. I got married there, my son was born there, and it became our home.

The land contract purchase helped me break into the homeownership market pretty without much risk. Along with sweat equity, I got a very nice home for very little money. By entering the housing market at such a low level, I lived in a house that was paid for free and clear, which allowed us to save as much money as possible and build up a savings very quickly.

Since we were living in a home with no mortgage and two paychecks, it did not take long for us to build up a comfortable amount of money for our future. The land contract was a very good way to break into homeownership, especially since I had very few assets. The owner was willing to be the bank, and he held the title to the property while I made monthly payments to him.

If I missed any payments to the owner, I would forfeit all the money I had given him. I would do a land contract again—but not without an attorney. Since then, I have had several types of mortgages. Securing a mortgage is similar to buying life insurance. Get the most money you can for the least amount coming out of your pocket on the front end at closing—and also in your monthly payments back to the lender. Mortgages and home equity loans can be very valuable in building your wealth. The next loan I took out was a construction loan.

Construction Loan

A construction loan is a loan you use to build a home with a builder. In my case, I was the contractor for my next home.

You determine the amount of money you are borrowing and the amount of time it will take to build the house. Once the amount of money and duration for construction have been established, you will get a book of checks to pay contractors for the work and materials they provide for the project.

The bank will send out an inspector to verify the level of completion to ensure that money is being spent in accordance with percentage of the work completed. If the inspector determines that 50 percent of the project is completed and you have not used 50 percent of the construction loan, that is a good thing. However, if you have spent 50 percent, and he determines that you are less than 50 percent complete, it could cause some serious problems for you (depending on how strict your lender is). You may have to apply for more money or more time—or both. I did not have any problems with this mostly because of my past experience in the building industry, but even if you have a builder doing all the work for you, the completion schedule could hold you up.

Choose a builder wisely. You will be billed monthly for the interest only on the money you use during the construction process. Every month, your interest charges grow. The longer it takes, the more interest you pay (no principal). If you have delays, it will cost you more, especially when you get to the very end. You will be paying a lot of interest until your house closes and rolls over into a conventional mortgage. If you have a bad builder, this could be an agonizing process.

When I wrote a check to a subcontractor to pay him for his services, he had to sign a waiver of lien. It stated that he had paid all his debts relating to my project so that no one could come back and put a lien on my project. This also applies if you are doing remodeling or repairs to a home with a conventional mortgage.

Imagine that I want to put in a new driveway. I find a paving contractor I want to work with, and we agree on a price to put in the driveway, including the concrete and labor. He does his job, and he wants his payment. Before you hand him a check, you will ask him to sign a waiver of lien to state that he has paid for everything related to this project.

Once everything is good, the kids are playing basketball on your new driveway. You get a knock at your door, and the concrete supplier hands you a lien on your house for the concrete he supplied. The contractor did not pay for it—even though he signed a paper saying that he did.

If the issue went to court, you would likely win due to the fact that the contractor perjured himself, but do you want to spend the time and money defending your innocence in court? On larger projects, you may get separate waivers of lien from the materials providers and the labor providers. This example falls under the terms of asset management or risk management. Preserving assets is just as important as acquiring them—and it is still under the veil of good stewardship.

When my construction loan was complete, we had to roll our loan from a construction loan to a conventional mortgage. The options are pretty standard across the lending/banking industry: thirty-year fixed, fifteen-year fixed, and adjustable-rate (usually in one-to-three-year increments) loans.

Thirty-Year Fixed Rate

At the time we were looking to put our newly built house into traditional financing, the thirty-year loan was the most popular. As the name says, the loan is paid back over thirty years. This loan is so popular with families because they can budget housing expenses over a long period of time while managing all the other expenses of raising a family. The monthly payments are generally lower due to the duration of the loan, but because of that long duration, you will pay interest on that money for a longer period of time.

Fifteen-Year Fixed Rate

This loan is locked in at an interest rate for fifteen years. Since the duration is shorter, the payments will be higher—even though you may get a little better interest rate. This loan has a more aggressive payment schedule, but the paydown on the loan is quicker. Fifteen years really goes by quickly. As long as you can manage the payment, this loan will be gone before you know it.

Most loans for commercial property will not go longer than fifteen years, and a higher down payment will be required. Currently, down payments for fifteen-year commercial loans vary between 20 and 30 percent. Home loans are now requiring more upfront money from borrowers. They all want more skin in the game (more of a commitment from borrowers).

Adjustable-Rate Mortgages

This is my favorite mortgage for several reasons, but it is not best for the family that is trying to get ahead and does not have a stable future or a secure long-term plan. I refinanced our home that was completely paid for because I wanted the money that was sitting in that house to contribute back to me through a new mortgage. Once I decided what I wanted to do with the money, I started to shop for a loan.

After my Saturday morning paper review of all the major home lenders, I found just what I was looking for: a three-year adjustable loan for 1.9 percent. The interest rate was locked in for three years with a one point cap per year, which meant the rate of interest could not go up more than 1 percent per year (3 points total). In three years, my loan wouldn't be any higher than 4.9 percent. If I wanted to lock in to the current interest rate before the end of my three-year loan duration, which more than likely would be higher but could be lower, I could pay $300 to lock in the current interest rate. With a feature like that, the adjustable-rate mortgage was perfect for my needs.

Most people cringe at the thought of interest rates going up on their borrowed money. In fact, most borrowers stay away from that type of loan, especially when they are trying to secure a budget for their family's expenses. However, for me, it is a wealth-building opportunity. The bank is offering me a loan at low interest rates to invest in high-yield securities with very little risk. An adjustable-rate loan could be beneficial for you if the low rates are somewhat stable—as they have been for the past ten years—or if you will only need money for a mortgage or other fiscal needs for a relatively short period of time.

Adjustable-rate loans are excellent and should not be overlooked as a loan option. Despite the potential volatility of interest rates, if you are raising a family and want expense stability, still consider an adjustable-rate loan. For the first three to five years, your payment goes straight to interest. It takes several years before you get the principal to start coming down. Why not shave a couple points off the most interest you will pay on the front end of your loan by going with a three-year adjustable loan? Do this for two cycles if rates are somewhat stable. When you are making a difference in your principal payback, refinance to a fixed-rate loan if it isn't a whole lot higher.

My current adjustable loan allows me to lock in the current rate for $300. Since my rate of 1.9 percent has only risen .5 percent, I will lock in the next three years at only a few dollars more on my monthly payment. I do not see interest rates rising so fast that I will want to refinance or even vanquish this loan.

Some people think it is a hassle to refinance after six years. Applying for a loan can be a giant pain. It is getting harder to get a mortgage, and there are a lot more conditions attached to it. Refinancing can be a hassle, but you will get plenty of notice if refinancing makes sense.

Do the math first. Are rates on the rise? What are the out-of-pocket costs to refinance? If you start with an adjustable-rate mortgage, the bank or lending institution might allow a conversion to a fixed-rate mortgage (for a fee). Be sure to ask before you sign. Many banks won't mention it. This approach could save you thousands in interest for a little bit of risk on the future of interest rates.

No one will look out for your money like you do. Being a

good steward of your money could easily give you more money to invest in your stock saving account. After forty years of paying mortgages, cutting grass, and looking back at what worked, what didn't work, and what it cost me in money and time, I would like to pass on my summarization of homeownership.

Society has programmed and conditioned us to feel like we really don't fit in unless we own a house. We don't appear somewhat successful unless we own a house. Other stereotypes program us to get an education, get a job, get married, or have children. These attributes and elements of society are not bad; in fact, they are good building blocks for our society. These values have made us a very strong country that we can be proud of.

The world views Americans as strong and affluent, but society is changing. We are generating more college-educated people and fewer tradespeople. Manual labor is not as desirable as white-collar professional careers. Those shifts in career choices bring a whole new set of standards about living and how the upcoming generations want to live, which has had an impact on the future of homeownership.

If I were to start over, I would have had a whole different criterion for owning a home. Owning a home is not an investment! It can potentially be a good financial move, but it is not an investment. It is an expense. The desire to have a large, beautiful home has been a big part of the American dream for close to one hundred years. It is part of our culture. Along with that culture, an element that has been pushed on us is that it is a bad thing to rent.

Homeownership might not be the driving force for the next generation. It is free time and mobility, and I don't know if that is such a bad thing. Freedom and mobility are things that I am trying to carve out more of in my life. Renting gives you much greater flexibility with your free time. There is no grass to mow, no household repairs, and no property taxes. Property taxes are built into your rent, but you don't have to write a separate check twice a year for them.

Renting can actually be an advantage if you are not certain where you want to settle down. If your career is still uncertain, renting can be a wise move financially. A friend of mine has taken the rental lifestyle to a very different and interesting level. He leases a hotel suite annually. He has made the suite his own with furnishings and artwork. He cooks his own meals in his full kitchen or goes downstairs to the hotel's restaurant. It is like condo living, but when his lease is up, he can leave with no further financial commitment. He pays for that flexibility with a higher monthly cost than conventional housing, but he has much greater options should his life suddenly change. Few of us can afford to live that lifestyle, and even fewer probably want that lifestyle, but more and more people are going for free time instead of long-term commitments.

The multifamily housing industry is on the rise, and single-family construction has been flat in comparison. Those trends run in about ten-year cycles, and they vary by geographical location. The baby boomers are downsizing. They want smaller places, more convenience, and a higher quality of life. There are many things to consider if you are trying to decide whether to rent or to own:

Location

Is housing affordable where you would like to live or need to live? About three-quarters of our country has affordable housing based on the mean income.

How Long Will You Stay in the Location?

If you are going to purchase a home, you should plan to stay a minimum of five years because the costs associated with purchasing a home are substantial. You will want to maximize the cost of purchasing and/or selling.

How Much House Can You Afford?

Here is my simple formula for building wealth: 10 percent to God, 15 percent to your investment savings, and 75 percent to live on. Out of that net income, I would spend no more than 25 percent on housing. Most real estate agents and financial planners will use 28 percent as the benchmark, and that is okay too. I just feel it is better to put your money where it works the hardest. An extra 3 percent in your stock saving will grow much faster than spending 3 percent more on a house. With my budget formula, you still have 50 percent of your net pay to support your lifestyle. This may or may not be easy for you, depending on how you like to live, but if you can live within this guideline, you will have money beyond your expectations.

Price-to-Rent Ratio

If your monthly rent for a house is below 15 percent, it is probably better to buy. If a $250,000 house rents for $3,000 per month, it is better to buy it:

$$\$3,000 \text{ per month} = \$36,000 \text{ per year}$$
$$\$36,000 \div \$250,000 = 14.4 \text{ percent}$$

Your mortgage will likely be less than $3,000 per month. It is a bit harder to calculate the price-to-rent ratio for an apartment, but based on the square footage, you should be able to compare an apartment cost to a house. If you are renting, it does not mean that you are throwing money away, especially if you are saving for yourself the way I have outlined. In fact, you can quite possibly be further ahead financially than if you owned a home.

Do not be fooled into thinking less of yourself if homeownership is not the lifestyle you want. It can actually provide more freedom, and more freedom equates to more free time. The time you spend researching and finding the best places to invest your money will reward you monetarily, and once your program is in place, it will provide you with more free time.

There is a ROI of your time as well. It is important to have a solid financial model in your life, but it is just as important—if not more important—to be mindful of how you spend your free time. With all your savings, assets, and all you accrue, you will not be able to buy more time. Spend your time carefully and wisely.

Vacation Home

My wife and I like to travel. We enjoy selecting, planning, and figuring out where we would like to spend our free time. We often thought that we would someday like to have our own getaway place for skiing or a place at the ocean. We first had an opportunity for a ski place three hours from home. We had gone there for years, and several friends had condos there. It was familiar and comfortable for us.

The first opportunity showed up for us at the same time I was buying my current office, and the price for both properties was the same. What a dilemma! A beautiful ski place—just remodeled and beautifully furnished—or an old farmhouse that needed a lot of work but was perfect for my company's growing needs. We felt very torn, and although we probably could have committed to both purchases, it was above and beyond our comfort level to extend ourselves that far out with two loans. Sadly, we passed on the fun purchase and went through with the office purchase.

Several years later, we took an offer from friends to visit them in their second home in the Baja Peninsula of Mexico on the Sea of Cortez. They had built their home more than twenty years ago in a small fishing village that still had dirt roads. We made the decision to take the plunge, fly to Cabo, rent a car, and drive to their home. We had never rented a car in Mexico, and although we had been to Mexico countless times over the past twenty years, we had never rented a car and driven through an unfamiliar country.

We were a little nervous about the short one-hour drive from the airport. The highway was nicely paved, but the lanes were narrow. There were not a lot of guardrails, and there were lots of steep ditches. About halfway to our destination, we encountered a roadblock of Mexican National Guard soldiers. They were stopping selected cars for inspection, which we assumed was for drug trafficking. We did not have to stop or even slow down.

Our cell phone went in and out of service, which made us a little nervous, but we finally made it to the little town on the east coast of the Sea of Cortez. There were dirt roads and cows and goats walking down the middle of Main Street. It was very underdeveloped. We met our friends, had lunch, and then went on a tour of the area.

To my surprise, my wife loved this rugged, throwback little town. I will never forget the look on her face after we stopped for breakfast the next day. We had ridden all over town, the beach, and a few points of interest.

I looked at her and said, "You love this place, don't you?"

She replied, "Oh yeah." Her smile could have melted an iceberg.

After that first visit, we made the journey to this little spot of heaven an annual event—sometimes biannually. We wanted to be there, and we started looking for a place. It didn't take long to find out that oceanfront property was $800,000 to several million. So much for oceanfront!

As with any oceanfront community, the farther you go from the shoreline, the lower the property values. In surveying the inventory of property for sale, we noticed a lot of half-built homes, garages, and lots with just a mobile home and a casita mixed into hillside neighborhoods. We wondered why that was. It looked like people ran out of money and just abandoned their projects. We soon learned the reason for such a wide range of homes: money.

As an American in Mexico, you cannot get a loan from a local bank. In America, you will not be able to secure a loan for a second home or get a construction loan in a foreign country. If you want to buy or build in Mexico, you better have a big bushel of cash. Our friends had a beautiful oceanfront home that they had owned for more than twenty years. They knew everything about the area, and they built from scratch, paying in cash as they went. They bought the lot for $20,000 and then started building. They made periodic trips to inspect the project and paid the contractor in cash as the work was completed.

There were some advantages to this method. By paying for completed work, it kept the contractor on the job. When the scheduled work wasn't completed, my friend would not release the cash. All in all, it was an enjoyable event for them. That would not work today. Bringing large amounts of cash into a foreign country is not advisable. In fact, if you bring more than $10,000 into a country from the United States, you are supposed to declare it before entering the country.

Once we had all the facts, we had hours of discussions and spent a lot of time looking at property and trying to figure out how to make it work. We entertained taking half-built garages, staying in a trailer on the property, or spending our vacations building a little retreat. We moved to the idea of buying something that was move-in ready and renting it when we weren't there.

After a lot of time looking at everything available (three or four times), my wife found one that spoke to her—very loud. To me, it was barely a whisper. It was only two blocks from the ocean. We could stand on the front porch and hear the ocean's roar. From the second-floor balcony, we could see the waves. It had issues, but my wife thought it was move-in ready. She said, "Let's go."

The Realtor told us the owner would finance it with a land contract, which got my attention. When you know something is right, you feel it. That was how Wendy felt about the house. We wanted to look at every option—the pluses and the minuses—and try to be objective about the whole deal.

After talking to several people, we discovered a local property-management firm that could handle everything from trimming the bushes to stocking the refrigerator with your favorite soda before you arrived. They were very capable and fair with their schedule of fees for the tasks provided. They knew every property in the area, and they told us that the property we were interested in could be rented easily for thirty to thirty-seven weeks per year. The rental income ranged from $1,200 per week to $2,000 per week, depending on the month (high season versus low season).

The additional bits of information gave us enough knowledge and courage to make an offer, but it was not to be. Try as we might, we could not come to terms with the owner and make it happen. We were both disappointed. My wife's visions of family and friends together on the Sea of Cortez in our own vacation home became a deconstructed dream.

If things don't come together or happen the way we hope for, we know there is a reason for it. For months, we talked about it. We even second-guessed our offer. Maybe we should have offered more or looked at a shorter-term land contract. We tried to figure out why the deal hadn't worked for us.

A few months later, we found out why it didn't happen. While we were trying to buy a place in that great little fishing village, our friends were trying to sell their home. Property values were at a sixteen-year low. They dropped the price from what they originally wanted and finally got a buyer without giving up a whole lot on the selling price. However, when it came to closing, the new owner got the keys, the Mexican bank held their money in escrow for what seemed like forever. They had to wait more than ten months to get their money. They were very frustrated about the whole ordeal. It was the opposite experience of building that home.

Our friends' experience selling their home gave us cause to reflect on what we would have totally overlooked had we not shared the experiences with them. It became very clear to us that we were not ready to own property in a country outside of the United States. Having an institution or government withhold assets in a nontransparent way is not desirable—even if it is in paradise.

God works in so many ways, and that was an example of how we need to watch for big and small signs. We had to think about all that was revealed and use wisdom before deciding. When something I want does not happen, it is for one of two reasons (or both). It doesn't happen because it is not good for you, the timing is wrong, you can't really afford it, or it may bring harm. If what you want doesn't happen, in most cases, it is because God has better plans for you.

When I was looking for my office building, my mother really wanted me to get one near my parents' house. She said, "Won't this be wonderful? You can come home, and I will fix you lunch."

Instead, I got something much, much better.

My mother recognized that it was better for me than having the chance to have lunch with her frequently.

Looking back at our desires to have a place in Mexico, I pieced together how it could have worked out. If we had paid cash for the house, it would have greatly depleted our nest egg. Our monthly earnings would have dropped too. The rental income would have offset the monthly drop in revenue—but not completely. If we had bought the house via land contract, the monthly payments would have been covered by the rental income with very little out-of-pocket expense, and our nest egg would have remained intact. That would have been the best scenario, but if we needed to sell, it could have taken more than a year to get out from under the commitment. It was more risk than I was willing to take.

My method of high-yield investing using compound interest will give you all the tools you need to construct whatever you would like. Our dream vacation spot may have not materialized for us at the time we were willing to go after it, but it wasn't because we didn't have the tools to make it happen. The timing was not right. Every month that goes by, we acquire more and more golden eggs by letting compound interest do its magic. With this in mind, I can rent a fabulous oceanfront home for a month or two—or even all year—and still keep the compound interest coming in and growing. It is much better to use the earnings to acquire whatever you want than to kill the goose that is laying the golden eggs.

The point of this wealth-building model is that you need the nest egg to generate the income stream. We have pretty much given up on owning a second home for the time being. Instead, we will enjoy ourselves in the parts of the world where we want to spend our time by renting—and then being able to walk away from any responsibilities that ownership has attached to it. In the meantime, our clutch of golden eggs keeps growing, which gives us more monthly income should the perfect homebuying opportunity come our way.

12

You Want to Stop Working Someday, Don't You?

36 golden eggs at 6 lbs. each = 216 lbs. per basket

97,977.6 grams @ $49.64 per gram = $4,863,608.00

One of the things that has given me much joy has been saving for retirement. For me, building a retirement account that would sustain my family throughout my time on earth was a huge challenge. It was much like training for and running a marathon. I have two siblings who run marathons. They both train for their races (contribution) by dedicating part of their days or weeks to training. When race day comes, they want to be ready, fit, and in the best possible shape to finish what they trained for. Once I realized that I would have to make my own retirement happen, the training had to start. Otherwise, I would not be able to run any marathon.

Once the savings toward a defined goal began to take shape, I saw definition. I was encouraged by my improvement, which made me want to do more. I wanted to take it to the max. I totally understand athletes who are training for an event or their personal goals. The adrenaline kicks in, and you just want to keep going.

In my readings about Warren Buffett, one very important characteristic comes to the surface about him. He is driven to do better—just as a runner wants to improve their finish time. For him, it is improvement, make it bigger and better, and watch it grow. His venue just happens to be money. This is part and parcel of the motivation that kept me focused to create a retirement and win the race.

Watching your investment grow—and watching almost anything grow—is exciting and encouraging. My method of high-yield investing helps maximize the laws of compound interest, which can help in two ways. The monthly cash can be used to reinvest and buy more high-yielding stocks that will make your dividends grow monthly, and if you couple it with monthly contributions (new money), you have just given rocket fuel to your compound interest machine. Secondly, and more importantly, once you have created this goose that lays golden eggs—and the monthly dividends become so substantial that you can see living on that monthly income—you will be heading into the retirement comfort zone.

Knowing that your monthly dividends are reaching your working income will give you peace of mind, but don't stop there. Keep rolling those dividends back into your machine. The snowball is going to get much bigger and much faster. The goal is to get an income stream from your retirement account without touching any of the principal.

My goal has been to have enough to be comfortable through

any economic climate, and this method provides that and more. It even works well in down markets, which always provide better buying opportunities. You may know someone with substantial wealth and think they don't need to worry because they have plenty of money. Money will not buy you happiness, but you don't want the lack of money to be the source of your misery, especially when you can do something to prevent it at the end of your life. A saving and investing plan can help you scratch the need for money off your list.

A very good friend who has great wealth, which he worked very hard for, finally decided to retire. We were discussing what he was going to do now that he has come into all the money and time that he could ever want.

He said, "When are you going to retire?"

I said, "I have no plans to ever stop working. I love what I am doing, and I can't wait to get into my office every day."

He said, "You have enough to retire on, don't you?"

I said, "Oh, yeah—and then some."

He asked, "How did you do it?"

"I started very young. In fact, I started the first year the personal IRA was enacted by Ronald Reagan in 1980." I can see it as if it happened yesterday. Ronald Reagan was on TV, and he was describing how the average American would now be able to save up personally for his own retirement.

"Reagan said, 'If Moses had started an IRA, just think about what kind of retirement he could have looked forward to."

Moses lived to be more than nine hundred years old. Wow! His IRA would have enough to retire our national debt, especially of he used my method of investing.

My friend said, "If I gave you a million dollars, show me how you would invest it on paper."

I wrote out a plan for him. After dividing up my selections, they would have netted about $180,000 annually (18 percent).

What he said about the investment plan after seeing it for the very first time was quite remarkable. "Investing this way gives you enough to live on, and as long as it does that, you don't need to worry about the principal value."

This is a great point. If you have what you need to live your life the way you want to live it, you won't have to worry if the market goes down (as long as your stocks keep paying). You will know their payment schedule every month because they declare it every month. You can see every month if there is a storm coming since forecasting is very easy.

Since I did that exercise on investing for my friend, I went back and compared my choices to the current prices of the same stocks. At the time of this writing, that model paid about 3 percent less—netting about $150,000 annually for a $1 million investment. The reason for the decrease in ROI is due to the drop in oil prices. One of the investments is an oil trust stock; lower oil prices bring lower dividends.

The market is a living, breathing thing, and it moves up and down. Although I set my investments on cruise control, I am always aware of the road ahead. I am always checking for hazards. Don't get caught asleep at the wheel.

Once your retirement accounts are generating the monthly income you desire—and you can see that this monthly income will afford you the lifestyle you want—it will be time to put another safeguard in place. Before you stop working and live solely on your retirement investments (and Social Security), having this safety net in place will help you achieve a worry-free retirement.

Determine your monthly dividends and then set aside half of them to be held in cash. Reinvest the other half to keep the account growing. Accrue enough cash to equal one year of your gross salary. This may take more than a year to achieve, but it is worth it as you go into retirement. This pile of cash is earning very little, but it is a tremendous tool should you need cash for an emergency.

My wife and I determined the amount of readily available cash we wanted for emergencies, and it took eighteen months of dividends to build a cache of reserve funds. If anything unexpected should happen, I have my own personal banker who I can call to help me with a situation—and that banker is me!

If you are fortunate enough to keep the investment snowball growing into retirement, it is not a bad idea to periodically add cash to your reserve. As you acquire more wealth, your need to have insurance for various reasons will diminish. You may have higher deductibles on your policies, which will lower your premiums. Depending on your comfort level and the amount of wealth you have acquired, you may be able to do away with certain types of insurance. My current term life insurance policy has a guaranteed premium for ten years at a very reasonable rate. When those rates expire, I will evaluate if it is cost-effective to keep buying it.

13

Everyone Needs an IRA!...
Not So Fast; You Can Hit The Lottery

I am now going to make a wild turn and explain how saving in an individual retirement account (IRA) is not as great for you and your family as it could be (talk about being a contrarian.) I can safely say that almost everybody has dreamed of hitting the lottery and what they would do with a large amount of unexpected cash: a new house, world travel, exotic cars, and pampering yourself beyond your wildest dreams. After that comes being generous to others, wiping out hunger in your hometown, funding a new addition to your church, and starting your own charity. Does any of that sound familiar?

Once you find out you hit the lottery, the first thing you have to decide is if you will take it in a lump sum or monthly payments. That is the whole point of this chapter. Is it better to have a nest egg or an income stream? Please think about that for a second before you answer.

I always felt that a lump sum was best for me because I knew that I would have no problem managing those funds in such a way that I could create more than if I waited to collect the money over a period of time. History has proven that, for the most part, people who are unfamiliar with large amounts of money generally do not manage money well.

While having large amounts of money is very comforting, the responsibility that comes with it can be overwhelming or even destructive if it is not managed properly. I have pointed out various examples of how money is the sharpest tool in your toolbox, and for those who get my message and dare to take advantage of my ways of investing, I have another approach to building wealth.

From the very beginning, I have strived to have a comfortable retirement, sacrificing in my youth so that I could enjoy life later. The very first year the personal retirement account came into being, I contributed the maximum allowed, and I continue to do that to this day. President Ronald Reagan's creation of the IRA has been one of the most significant wealth builders for the working man to create a nest egg for his golden years since Social Security.

Social Security was created as a supplement to the working man's retirement. It was never meant to be a sole source of income for retirement. The IRA has also been a large contributing factor to the growth of the stock market because we want something more substantial in the way of seeing our money grow besides sitting in a bank, which provides security but very little growth.

For more than thirty-five years, our working population has had the idea that they have to take a commanding role in their own retirement destiny. I have been the poster child for this, and it is working as designed because I took an active role to achieve the results I wanted. Social Security will be a supplement to my retirement as it was intended; in fact, it will totally be play money for me. My goal was to have that nest egg at the end to provide for my family's needs and my heart's desires. It worked. I hit my own lottery. I have my lump sum, my nest egg. I could have done it much better if I had paid more attention to the bigger picture at the finish line—and the pothole on the other side of the finish line is income taxes.

With all qualified money (except for the Roth IRA), every bit of tax-deferred money you take out of an IRA or 401(k) will be taxed as ordinary income, which is the highest level of taxes. The level of tax depends on your total income for the year. As an example, I will use a 30 percent rate of taxation. When the government set up this program, it was providing a tax deferral of the money you set aside at the time of deposit on the premise that the money can keep growing unencumbered by taxes, which is true and a good thing. However, when you start taking the money out, you will have to pay the tax on all that growth—as if it were your paycheck. In itself, that isn't really a bad thing, but what isn't mentioned—and what most people don't realize—is that most people make the most money at the very end of their careers, which puts them in higher tax brackets. The kids are gone and out of college, the house is paid for, your careers are generally peaking because you're much wiser about almost everything. You make fewer mistakes about almost everything; therefore, you have more.

The government allowed this plan to be opened up for working masses because it provided a way to save up for ourselves, making us less dependent on Social Security. That could allow the government to dial down the debt that Social Security created, and it provided government coffers with higher tax bracket contributors. It was a win-win situation (in theory) just like Social Security, but it never quite worked as planned because they can't leave a good thing alone. They have to fix it.

Nevertheless, there is more good than bad about the IRA. You're taking out money from your IRA nest egg, and all the money you take out will be taxed as ordinary income, exactly the same as your paycheck. For every dollar you take out of your IRA, you pay Uncle Sam thirty cents (using the 30 percent tax bracket), which is one-third of all your retirement cash taken out. That really sucks.

I have a much better approach that will use the strategies in this book to provide the same compounding principles with only half of the tax liability, which will provide you with at least a 15 percent increase in your wealth management. This is a proof-positive example that can be applied to your goals today and started at any time throughout your retirement saving career. Of course, the sooner it is started, the better—and the younger, the better.

Let's use $1 million as the size of the nest egg you want for retirement. The financial planners of the world tell us we should never run out of money if we take out 4 percent of our retirement (this isn't my guideline, but I see what they are trying to get at). I will use 5 percent because I think it is more in line with people's spending. 5 percent of $1 million is $50,000 taxed at 30 percent is $15,000.

$$\$1,000,000 \times .05 = \$50,000 \times 30 \text{ percent} =$$
$$\$15,000 \text{ taxes to be paid on } \$50,000$$
$$\$50,000 - \$15,000 = \$35,000$$

By taking out 30 percent out of the $50,000 for income taxes, your net is $35,000, which equates to $2,916.66 per month. If you are happy with $3,000 a month plus whatever Social Security pays you per month, I am very happy for you. Personally, I did not work hard my entire life to have a $3,000 per month payout at retirement. If that is all that I could accumulate for retirement, it is one thing, but to have Uncle Sam take one-third of my retirement savings seems almost criminal.

You might think I am painting an unrealistic picture by using 30 percent tax bracket for a $50,000 income, but most people have other income that has to be considered at tax time.

If you would like to see a purer example, let's use a 20 percent tax bracket.

$$\$1,000,000 \times .05 = \$50,000 \times 20 \text{ percent} =$$
$$\$10,000 \text{ taxes to be paid on } \$50,000$$
$$\$50,000 - \$10,000 = \$40,000$$

This will net you about $400 more per month ($3,333.33 versus $2,916.66). Even at a 20 percent tax rate, your monthly net income is like being paid $20 per hour. It doesn't seem right to have this tax burden as we become seniors and drop out of the workforce.

This paints a very realistic picture of the tax rate you can expect to pay when you start taking out the money you saved for retirement. I have a much better way. Let's take that same million-dollar nest egg, but instead of having it in a qualified savings account (another name for a retirement account), you save all that money in an ordinary stock trading account (the kind described earlier in this book).

Let's apply my investment strategies to this $1 million lump sum. Since my investments generate between 13 and 18 percent, I will use my standard 15 percent return on investment. Let's do the math.

$$\$1,000,000 \times 15 \text{ percent} = \$150,000$$

This $1 million generates $150,000 in dividends per year, but the beautiful part here is the tax liability on the $150,000 is 15 percent because these dividends are in the tax category of capital gains, which is close to half of the earned income rate.

$$\$150,000 \times 15 \text{ percent capital gains}$$
$$\text{rate} = \$22,500 \text{ tax liability}$$
$$\$150,000 - \$22,500 = \$127,500 \text{ income}$$
$$\text{free and clear } (\$10,625 \text{ per month})$$

This is a much better way to approach retirement than using qualified accounts. This income stream is better than the lump sum nest egg, which you carve away at and pay more taxes— even with the tax deferral you get while saving in the qualified account. In fact, the tax deduction is paltry compared to the savings you get by paying capital gains along the way as you sock money away.

If you are committed to saving for retirement in a qualified retirement account, how is saving in a stock account any different? If you will be committed to putting money aside for an IRA or 401(k), it should not be a problem to put the same amount of money in a different bucket that will grow at the same rate. It just has a different label.

I am on the threshold of retirement, and I am planning how and when I will take my retirement funds. If I could do it over, I would do it differently. I would do it better with lower taxes, which really does make it better. The only retirement account I would have is a Roth IRA because no taxes are associated with it. A large low-tax income stream can provide you the best possible cash-rich retirement. When dealing with your money, you need to write down where all of your money comes and goes.

If you haven't done it in a while, you should sit down and do that to refresh your goals. Every six months, I take a snapshot of what I have coming in, and it still amazes me how compound interest makes your money grow. When you create a budget, be sure to allocate an allowance to go into stock savings accounts and an amount for retirement, but do not put that money into an IRA account yet.

If you already have a traditional IRA, I would convert it to a self-directed stock Roth IRA. Depending how much you have and where you are in your savings, you may have to pay income tax on the conversion. Check with your tax advisor on your tax liability to get into a Roth. If the principal loss of your IRA conversion is more than 15 percent, I would not convert your IRA to a Roth IRA. I would also stop contributing to the regular IRA and open a Roth IRA.

Let's look at this saving program as if we were starting from scratch. The first thing to do is list all of your fixed expenses, all of your income, and all of your goals. These things together may not balance out. Having too many fixed expenses for your income would be the most common cause for people not being able to achieve their goals. You should adjust to balance these three things.

Try to reduce your fixed expenses and eliminate any expenses you absolutely do not need. Credit card debt is usually the most common culprit. Avoid dining out. Don't stop every morning for that foamy latte that you treat yourself to. Pack your lunch instead of going out every day. (I still eat leftovers for lunch.) Get some extra income. Sell things that you are not using anymore. Even if it is pennies on the dollar, the cash can be put to work helping the compound interest machine as opposed to collecting dust in your closet. If you have time, work an extra part-time job or work overtime and dedicate all the extra cash to your stock savings program. You are feeding the goose that lays golden eggs.

I would allocate my monthly income in a simple, straightforward way that absolutely guarantees results:

10 percent to charity (tithing)
15 percent to a stock savings account
75 percent to pay bills, pay down debt, and have fun

Depending on where your disciplines lie, you may think you can't possibly do that. You may think you have too many expenses to give away 10 percent and save 15 percent. It is more than possible. If you commit to it by giving to God and getting out of debt, you will be able to save more than 15 percent for yourself. This will not be easy, but it is a worthwhile goal. It will take lots of discipline and training. It may be difficult at first—or even seem impossible—but this savings plan will provide abundance. It is a promise from God.

Once you commit to this monthly ritual, it will become automatic. Here is a trick to help streamline your efforts: Once your budget is firmly in place, have your paycheck direct-deposited into your stock savings account—and then have your largest budget allocations taken out of your account automatically (mortgage, car payments, and credit card payments). By doing this, you will be on autopilot, and you will not have to remember to pay a bill. It also helps build your credit score because your major bills will always be paid on time.

Having one account that you can use to do everything—save, automatically pay bills, write checks, and buy stocks—keeps everything centralized. If you have extra money one month, you can invest it right along with your 15 percent monthly high-yield stock purchases. If you need some emergency cash, no transferring of funds will be needed. Just write a check!

Once you have a stock savings account, what are the mechanics of this worry-free investment model; would you rather have an income stream or a nest egg? This financial model, this way of saving and investing, and this way of living provide you with both. It provides all the elements for a balanced financial life. Giving plus saving plus spending equals an abundant, well-balanced financial life.

An unbalanced financial life can be one of the most uncomfortable journeys in life. Financial imbalance reaches some of the farthest parts of our perceived well-being, but it does not have to. This model is simple, the principles are easy to understand, and the results are proven. Compound interest is the greatest wealth builder anyone can put to use. Albert Einstein said that compound interest is the strongest force in the universe.

Let's use an example for my savings model with a gross salary of $75,000 per year (about $37 per hour) and a tax rate of 28 percent that will net about $54,000 per year.

$$\$75,000 \times 28 \text{ percent} = \$21,000$$
$$\$75,000 - \$21,000 = \$54,000 \div 12 =$$
$$\$4,500 \text{ per month net pay}$$

Divide the $4,500 net pay into my allocations:

Give 10 percent = $450
Saving 15 percent = $675
Spend 75 percent = $3,375

This is a very balanced allocation of a modest salary; 25 percent of your salary is dedicated, and 75 percent is flexible to be spent on your lifestyle. In our example, we will take this savings plan out five years and see what happens.

Example 1

In our savings example, like the bowl of rice example, the compound interest does not appear that growth is all that significant, but by the end of the first year, we are getting close to $100 per month on monies put into savings. By the end of the fifth year, the interest earned per month exceeds your contribution ($729.26 – $675 = $54.26) by a little more than $50. This is only after five years!

After only five years, the contribution to your savings account each month has doubled! Your contribution of $675 each month plus a minimum of $729.26 brings your contributions up to $1,404.26, which is a fabulous rate of growth for your savings, your lump sum, and your nest egg. The nest egg is now generating more of an income stream than your contribution.

Example 1

1ST YEAR $8,100 SAVED $500.95 INT	2ND YEAR $16,200 SAVED $2,556.96 INT	3RD YEAR $24,300 SAVED $$6,121.03 INT
J $675.00	J $8,680.75 + $108.51 + $675	J $18,756.96 + $234.46 + $675
F $675.00 + $8.44 + $675	F $9,464.26 + $118.51 + $675	F $19,666.42 + $245.83 + $675
M $1,358.44 + $16.98 + $675	M $10,257.56 + $128.22 + $675	M $20,587.25 + $257.34 + $675
A $2,050.42 + $25.63 + $675	A $11,060.78 + $138.26 + $675	A $21,519.59 + $269 + $675
M $2,751.05 + $34.39 + $675	M $11,874.04 + $148.43 + $675	M $22,463.58 + $280 + $675
J $3,460.44 + $43.26 + $675	J $12,697.47 + $158.72 + $675	J $23,419.37 + $292.74 + $675
J $4,178.70 + $52.23 + $675	J $14,375.33 + $179.69 + $675	J $24,387.11 + $304.84 + $675
A $4,905.93 + $61.32 + $675	A $15,230.02 + $190.38 + $675	A $25,336.95 + $316.71 + $675
S $5,642.25 + $70.53 + $675	S $15,230.02 + $190.38 + $675	S $26,328.66 + $$329.11 + $675
O $6,387.78 + $79.85 + $675	O $16,095.40 + $201.19 + $675	O $27,332.77 + $341.66 + $675
N $7,142.63 + $89.28 + $675	N $16,971.59 + $212.14 + $675	N $28,349.43 + $354.37 + $675
D $7,906.91 + $98.83 + $675	D $17,858.73 + $223.23 + $675	D $29,378.73 + $367.23 + $675

4TH YEAR $32,400 SAVED $11,592.07 INT	5TH YEAR $40,500 SAVED $19,244.74 32% OF ACCOUNT VALUE
J $30,421.03 + $380.26 + $675	J $43,992.07 + $549.90 + $675
F $31,476.29 + $393.45 + $675	F $45,216.97 + $549.90 + $675
M $32,544.74 + $406.81 + $675	M $46,457.18 + $580.71 + $675
A $33,626.55 + $420.33 + $675	A $47,712.89 + $596.41 + $675
M $34,721.88 + $434.02 + $675	M $48,984.30 + $612.30 + $675
J $35,830.90 + $447.89 + $675	J $50,271.60 + $628.40 + $675
J $36,953.70 + $461.92 + $675	J $52,575 + $644.69 + $675
A $38,090.71 + $476.13 + $675	A $52,894.69 + $661.18 + $675
S $39,241.84 + $490.52 + $675	S $54,230.87 + $677.89 + $675
O $40,407.36 + $505 + $675	O $55,583.76 + $694.80 + $675
N $41,587.45 + $519.84 + $675	N $56,953.56 + $711.92 + $675
D $42,782.29 + $534.78 + $675	D $58,340.48 + $729.26 + $675

$59,744.74

$40,500 SAVED IN 5 YEARS

$19,244.74 INTEREST

system malfunction
please contact:
Chaney Digital sign
and catering

Our next example shows how the magic of compound interest works even if you stop contributing to your nest egg. This example includes reinvesting the dividends every year.

Example 2

Even without contributing any additional monies to this saving machine, the laws of compounding keep generating money. By dumping the dividends back into your investments, you will end up close to $1 million for a nest egg. The best part of all is that the nest egg generates an income stream of almost $150,000 annually, which equals $12,500 per month. That is incredible when you consider that you have only contributed $40,500 to this model.

If you start this savings plan at age twenty-five, stick to it, stop contributing to it after five years, and let it go on its own for the next twenty years—just being mindful to keep the earnings going back into the savings model—you will be a millionaire by the time you are fifty years old. That is fifteen years before retirement age.

If you can commit to this model, the results will be greater and more of a sure thing than winning the lottery.

In example 2, we did not show monthly investment (only annual investments). To shorten the example, if it is an exact calculation, your nest egg will actually be bigger because you will have monthly compounding, which was not calculated in our example. Therefore, you will have more, which is even more of a reason to do the savings task monthly. The tax liability on your dividends is not mentioned in this example, and at 15 percent, it will have an impact on your saving machine if you have to pay the taxes out of those earnings. In example 2, we show no contributions to the savings model. You should have enough somewhere else to cover your tax liability on the savings machine.

The nest egg amount will not be as great after twenty years due to the fact that your investment holdings constantly change in value. If your holdings go down in value, but they still pay the same dividends, the percentage paid goes up. You are not losing on your investment. When shares of stock go down in value, it is an opportunity to buy more dividend-producing shares at a discount. The income stream has always been more important to me than the value of the nest egg, but you don't get income stream without the nest egg.

The income stream in this example will probably be larger than your take-home pay. If you choose to, you will have more than $12,000 per month at your disposal. That is pretty incredible, especially when you consider that you stopped putting money into this savings model after only five years ($40,500).

One huge point needs to be driven home here. If you started this program at age twenty-five, you will be a millionaire by fifty. Most of the hard work and sacrifice was at the front end (in the first five years). After that, you are on autopilot. With a million-dollar nest egg (plus or minus) and an income stream of $150,000 per year, which is taxed at only 15 percent, why do you want or need an IRA?

The taxes on the IRA when taken out are at an earned-income rate (same as a paycheck). It is foolish to give Uncle Sam an extra 13 to 15 percent when you don't have to. Even using this savings model within an IRA, which I did to get the law of compound interest working for me, I am faced with paying the higher tax upon using any of the money interest or principal when I go to take any of that money.

The financial industry pundits will tell you that an IRA is the best way to ensure a comfortable retirement.

To that, I say, "Poppycock!"

They will tell say, "You get a tax deduction for your contribution!"

Big deal! If we use the same gross income to calculate the tax savings, you will see that it is paltry in tax savings off your tax liability. The tax deduction of $4,000 off of a gross income of $75,000 looks something like this:

$$\$75{,}000 - \$4{,}000 = \$71{,}000$$
$$\$75{,}000 \times 28 \text{ percent} = \$21{,}000$$
$$\$71{,}000 \times 28 \text{ percent} = 19{,}880$$
$$\$21{,}000 - \$19{,}880 = \$1{,}120$$

This is oversimplified since other deductions will make up a more cumulative tax deduction (mortgage interest, medical expenses, etc.). The little bit of deduction on the front end does not justify the larger tax at the end.

Example 2

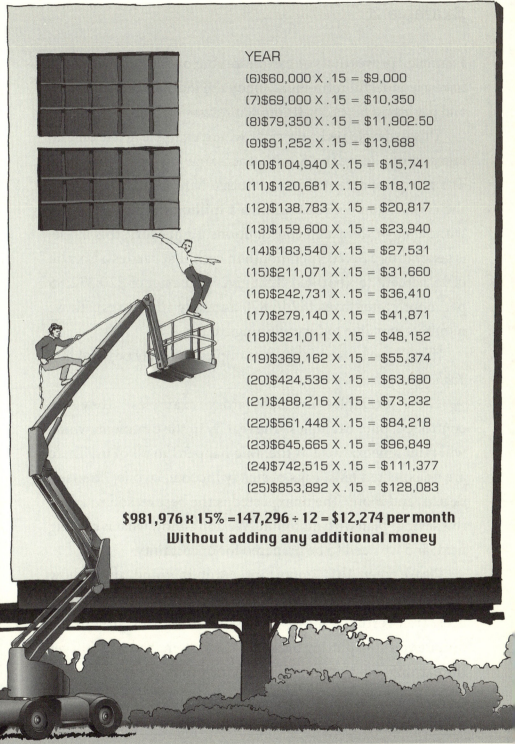

YEAR

(6)$60,000 X .15 = $9,000

(7)$69,000 X .15 = $10,350

(8)$79,350 X .15 = $11,902.50

(9)$91,252 X .15 = $13,688

(10)$104,940 X .15 = $15,741

(11)$120,681 X .15 = $18,102

(12)$138,783 X .15 = $20,817

(13)$159,600 X .15 = $23,940

(14)$183,540 X .15 = $27,531

(15)$211,071 X .15 = $31,660

(16)$242,731 X .15 = $36,410

(17)$279,140 X .15 = $41,871

(18)$321,011 X .15 = $48,152

(19)$369,162 X .15 = $55,374

(20)$424,536 X .15 = $63,680

(21)$488,216 X .15 = $73,232

(22)$561,448 X .15 = $84,218

(23)$645,665 X .15 = $96,849

(24)$742,515 X .15 = $111,377

(25)$853,892 X .15 = $128,083

**$981,976 x 15% = 147,296 ÷ 12 = $12,274 per month
Without adding any additional money**

Example 3

Example 3 proves that you can create your own lottery winnings, have a wonderful retirement, enjoy the journey along the way, and pay less in taxes on all your winnings—all without an IRA.

This example picks up right where example 1 left off and takes it out to year 25 with the same savings procedure. The most important thing to notice here is that by staying the course, you will end up with a million-dollar nest egg—without any increase in contributions. At age fifty, this model is generating $24,203 per month in cash that carries a tax rate of 15 percent ($3,630.45). That gives you a net of $20,572.55 per month after taxes ($246,870 annually after taxes). Those numbers look like lottery winnings to me.

If you have looked at these examples, you may be thinking, *Yeah right!*

These examples are laboratory examples. They are controlled, pure examples. The real fly in the ointment, which will taint any example, is life. Life happens to all of us. There are unexpected bills, gaps of steady income, layoffs, illnesses, deaths, and more. The unexpected is the best reason to adopt this savings plan with discipline. We don't know what is coming next, and we need to be prepared for uncertainty.

Please keep this important point in mind about how compound interest works. Any interruption of the investment cycle (reinvesting your dividends) will stop this growth the minute you stop putting back into the system. You will still get the earning, but the growth cycle stops cold.

Example 3

YEAR

(6)$60,000 + $8,100 + $10,215
(7)$78,315 + $8,100 + $12,962
(8)$99,377 + $8,100 + $16,122
(9)$123,599 + $8,100 + $19,755
(10)$151,454 + $8,100 + $23,933
(11)$183,487 + $8,100 + $28,738
(12)$220,325 + $8,100 + $34,264
(13)$262,689 + $8,100 + $40,618
(14)$311,407 + $8,100 + $47,926
(15)$367,433 + $8,100 + $56,330
(16)$431,863 + $8,100 + $65,995
(17)$505,950 + $8,100 + $77,109
(18)$591,167 + $8,100 + $89,890
(19)$689,157 + $8,100 + $104,589
(20)$801,845 + $8,100 + $121,492
(21)$931,437 + $8,100 + $140,930
(22)$1,080,468 + $8,100 + $163,285
(23)$1,251,853 + $8,100 + $188,993
(24)$1,448,946 + $8,100 + $218,557
(25)$1,675,603 + $8,100 + $252,555

$1,936,250 X 15% = $290,439
$290,439 ÷ 12 MONTHS = $24,203 PER MONTH

14

Should I Stay or Should I Go...
Social Security, when to take it?

The baby boomer generation is posed to inherit $4 trillion from our parents. This makes us the wealthiest generation to ever walk the earth. That is probably a good thing for most boomers, and the simple reason is that boomers are spenders and not savers.

I recently read a shocking statistic: 70 percent of all boomers have less than $100,000 saved up for retirement. That is a very scary thought, and I wonder how many have the attitude that their inheritance will get them through retirement. Our parents' generation were savers and not spenders due to the fact that many of them grew up in the Great Depression. That experience ingrained fear in them that carried through their lives, including their golden years. They also wanted to make it better for their children than they had it.

Another of my contrarian views is about when to take Social Security. I will have to make this decision very soon. I can take at age sixty-two (which will be in two months at the time of this writing). I can wait until age sixty-six and get 33 percent more every month. I can also wait until age seventy and get 52 percent more.

At first blush, it looks like a no-brainer to wait until seventy and take a bigger monthly payout. I will agree with that reasoning with two conditions in mind. If you will definitely need that money as part of your retirement income, you will need to work longer and retire later in life. The second reason to wait longer is your health. If you are in good health, then there is no reason you can't work longer and gain the larger monthly check.

When I received my account statement from Social Security, I thought, *Wow! If I wait until seventy, I will get more than double what I would get if I take it at sixty-two.*

I'm very healthy, and I don't plan to quit working because I love what I do and the people I work with. Why take the money in a few months? Because cash is king—and it is another way for me to get money!

I took my monthly money from Social Security and applied it to my investment model, using 12 percent compound interest to my investment contributions. Was it better for me to take Social Security at sixty-two, sixty-six, or seventy? How many years will I be able to take Social Security before my departure? Nobody knows when that time will come, but you can use average life expectancies to give you an estimation. I used the age of ninety because I feel it will take me that long to get my work done. The other interesting fact I found out by doing this exercise is that if I take Social Security at sixty-two, it will take only eight years for me to take out everything I contributed to my account. I plan to work past sixty-two, which means there will be a limit on the earnings I can make without being taxed—plus the Social Security will still be taken out of my salary.

In essence, I will be putting money back into the system. I will be helping to pay my Social Security distribution. I am okay with that because I am using that money early to help build yet another income stream, but what happens next?

Here is how my quest for another income stream via Social Security shook out for me. Thirty days before I turned sixty-two, I applied for benefits online. It thought it was going to be a nightmare, but it was extremely easy and quick. One of the questions was if I planned to work after benefits were initiated. I plan to work full-time after starting benefits, and since I really don't need this income to live on—and even though I would have paid additional income tax on it—my thought was to create another golden egg-laying goose to add to my compound interest generating model.

It took a few minutes for them to acknowledge my application and let me know they would be getting back to me soon about my journey into retirement. In less than a week, I received a phone call from a benefits counselor. It was a Sunday afternoon, and it seemed odd to call over the weekend. She was very polite and very knowledgeable about the system, and she proved to me that it was certainly in my best interests to wait to take benefits until I was sixty-six. At that time, I would be able to work as much as I wanted and make as much money as I wanted without any adverse effects on my benefits with regard to additional taxes. The monthly benefits would be 35 percent higher, and it would only take about nine years for me to exhaust the amount of money that I contributed to this government annuity. Fortunately, I'm not in need of this income, and the system wouldn't have to pay out the money for another four years. The Social Security system, in concept, is a very good thing. It helps people who need help, but it is in disrepair for several reasons. Most of them are political, which is a subject I won't touch. This is really poor stewardship by the people we elect to watch over these things. Does that make us just as guilty as the people we elect?

The system has more takers than givers. By design, that has always been the case. I read in college that the first beneficiary of Social Security lived to receive more than $20,000 in benefits while only contributing a little more than $2 to her account. While that is a factor, I don't believe it is the major reason for the problem. If the money that has been collected over the amount of time had been invested to create an additional income stream into the system, using compound interest to work for the system—even if the goals for ROI were set much lower than what I have outlined in this book—Social Security could be very healthy and not on the verge of running out of money by 2034.

The second factor hurting the system is the birth rate of our nation is very close to zero growth; for every person who dies, one person is born. This means there is no growth for contributions to the insurance policy run by our government. There are so many additional thoughts, reasons, and theories why Social Security is in trouble, but you should take responsibility with all the assets that pass through your hands to construct a continuous asset stream wherever you can— even using these funds that will come your way at retirement through Social Security.

If you have a good retirement plan that can afford you and your family the lifestyle you want, you are certain that you won't run out of funds midway through retirement, and you are ready to stop working or at least working for a paycheck, then you are a great candidate for taking Social Security as early as possible. If you are in this very strong position, then those monthly contributions coming in can be very flexible and life enhancing.

What is more important—and in many ways more precious—than this extra money is your free time. Not being accountable to someone else, a job, or a meeting is a freedom that everyone who has toiled most of their adult lives should get to experience. Social Security was designed to provide everyone some additional supplements to contributors at the end of their working day—not a total retirement plan.

The other candidate who should take Social Security at sixty-two or as early as it makes sense is the person with health problems or life-shortening conditions. Get that money coming into you as soon as you can. It's yours—put it to use in the best way you can. If at all possible, try to put some of this newfound money to work with the compound interest magic outlined in this book.

Social Security is a living, breathing thing, and like many other things, it started out as a great idea and ended up as a quagmire, which totally proves my father's theory that no one will look out for your money like you do. When you approach your sixties, start to take a closer look at your financial situation with regard to taking so that you can plan retirement. Social Security will send statements to help you see your status within the system, which will assist you in making the right choice.

My Social Security advisor stressed applying for Medicare one month before you turn sixty-five! That is a totally separate procedure from Social Security, but it is an important enhancement for a comfortable retirement.

15

Don't Go Until You Get Your Paperwork Done

Being a loving, responsible head of a family has so many facets and elements that it sometimes makes me wonder why we haven't gone the way of the dinosaurs. Our society seems to be eating away at core family values. This cannibalistic feeding on each other makes it harder and harder on parents to start and raise families to completion. Divorce is commonplace. I have experienced it firsthand, and it attacked my family unit.

In the fifties, divorce seemed so rare. If I had to guess, I would say that one in one hundred families was a broken home. Today, it seems like a marriage that remains intact for thirty years is more and more a rarity. These days, planning for a family's sovereignty is more difficult. With splintered and fragmented family units, it is more important than ever to be prepared to care for the members of your family should an unplanned early departure happen.

The best way to provide for your family and yourself is to have an income stream from your investments. Once that investment plan is in place and working, it can be set on autopilot to keep growing, but you will still need another layer of protection to transfer all the risks of death. Another way to transfer that risk of death is to buy insurance.

Life insurance is an important part of our stewardship in raising a family. There are so many types of life insurance out there to choose from, including whole life and universal life. The only one I will expound on is term life insurance. Early in my young adult life, when I was gearing up to be a family man, I had a very wealthy client who I could consult with about anything financial. It only took about ten minutes for him to convince me which type of life insurance would be the best choice.

Term insurance only pays if you die. There is no cash value, and the premiums are the lowest of all the life insurances. Any of life insurances that provide a cash value are more expensive for the same amount of death benefit. You will have to hold that policy for many years before you accrue any cash value. If you have a whole life policy, it may take ten years for the cash value to show up on your policy statement.

You will have paid an extra amount of money into that policy for ten years—only to see the cash value be a fraction of what you paid above the cost of term insurance. The only people accruing wealth on your insurance policies are the insurance companies and the agents who sold you the policies.

If the agent is your brother, and you want to help him out with his new career, that's great! Help him out! Buy him a new suit—but don't but a whole life insurance policy from him (maybe buy him this book). If you buy the term life insurance policy, invest the cost difference between term and whole life policies. You will beat any actuary tables the insurance company shows you for how your policy grows in value. Only buy term life insurance!

Everyone Needs a Will

Andrew Carnegie's mother said, "You came into this world with nothing—and you are going to leave with nothing." She was trying to shame him into leaving his money to charity. What she said is quite true, but there is more to it than that, especially because of the enormous wealth that he acquired during his stay on earth.

You can't take it with you either, and having a will fits into a model of good stewardship. Since you can't take it with you, you will need to figure out where all your stuff goes and/or who gets it. A will is a written document that lets the world know what you want done with your possessions after your life on earth ends.

By having a will, you are being responsible to the people you love and care about: family, friends, and charities. With a will, you can spell out exactly how you would have assets, possessions, and final actions carried out. A will should be a priority, especially if there are minor children in your family. Who will be their caretakers should both parents have an untimely demise? Their guardians should be spelled out; otherwise, the court system will appoint someone to fill that role.

Along with your will, make sure that you have a living will that spells out your wishes with regard to medical situations that require external life-support systems. You should also have someone who you can appoint to have power of attorney on your behalf. This person can sign papers on your behalf, make financial arrangements, and assist you with most legal matters.

A will should be considered an important part of your family's protection. It is like buying an insurance policy to cover the costs of your funeral. It spells things out using your words, your directions, and—ideally—settles matters peacefully for your beneficiaries. Money and things do strange things to people. Siblings fight over their parents' things that may or may not be spelled out in a will. When you are writing out your will, add the following line: "Should anyone named in this will contest its content, they will receive nothing—and their portion will go to charity."

Trusts

If you own a home and have children, you need a trust! A trust is a legal implement to convey property and/or funds to a trustee by a trustor for the beneficiary (your heirs). There are so many types and ways to create a trust that you will need to investigate what will work for your wants and needs.

I researched trusts for more than a year before I jumped in. I read more than six books on the subject and still had to have my trust tailor-made to my needs and wants. There are many benefits of a trust. A trust, unlike a will, avoids going through probate court.

When my grandmother passed away, my mother and my aunt received all my grandmother's assets, home, money, and possessions. The court tied up the execution of the will for eighteen months. It took a year and half to settle a simple will, and the longer it takes, the more you are going to pay in attorney fees.

When my father passed away, his simple will transferred everything to my mother—effortlessly and quickly. My accountant, who was also a close friend, highly recommended creating a trust for all my mother's assets for a couple of reasons. If my mother became ill, the trust would be responsible for taking care of her. The four children who were beneficiaries of her estate would have everything seamlessly transferred to them as surviving members of a will—with no probate. When my mother passed away, the trust passed on to my three siblings and me without any glitches.

The effort and expense you put in at the front end can pay back dividends. The last thing you want or need when your family is in a time of grief is to have legal issues settling up, putting closure to the details that come with the passing of a family member.

Along with a will, a trust should be considered an extra veil of protection for avoiding the entanglements of the courts.

PART 4

Wait... There's More (Aww... Come On)

16

HSA, Health Saving Account

In the late nineties, I was starting my life over and reconstructing all the elements required to function. I also realized I had no health insurance. As I was searching for high-yield stocks with my father, we were discussing how I could have health insurance that wouldn't cost me an arm and a leg.

We saw an ad in the *Wall Street Journal* for a new health insurance program called a health savings account (HSA). The ad described it as medical insurance along with a savings account to pay medical bills: a high deductible, a low premium, and the benefits of a tax deduction. It was marketed as a new type of medical insurance plan that specifically helped small businesses and the self-employed.

The federal government was only going to allow 750,000 of these plans to be issued. After checking into the program, I discovered that it was definitely a good fit. The great thing for me was that the premiums were low, but that came with a high deductible. This was also a good fit for me because I was healthy. The really great part of plan was that I could have a savings account that I could contribute to before taxes, take the tax deduction, and use the money to pay for medical expenses tax-free.

The maximum contribution was $3,900 per year, and out of those tax-free funds, you could pay for anything related to health care. What a great plan! You can build up a medical-needs nest egg for emergencies and use it to pay your high deductible if you need to go to the hospital. It can be used to buy medicine, eyeglasses, or even aspirin or bandages, but it cannot be used to pay monthly premiums.

An additional benefit to an HSA is that the money can be rolled into your regular IRA once you have signed up for Medicare. I'm sure the architects of this plan feel that very few people will have any money to roll over into their IRA after using the money for health care. This society does not encourage saving money.

This plan encourages people to save for themselves with regard to health care, and if it catches on, it could lessen the burden on government-funded health care. Once I got all the facts about an HSA, I jumped on board and got it for myself and my dependents. It was the perfect medical coverage system for our needs and affordability, and it satisfied my interest in setting aside more money for emergencies.

After a few years in the plan, I had an idea. If I could put my HSA savings into a self-directed stock program, then I could apply my investment model of compounding interest to this medical savings money. After much searching, I found one HSA institution in the entire country that allows self-directed investing. I'm not certain if that is still the case, but it has been an excellent way to grow my medical savings account in the same seamless, successful way as my other investment system.

Regardless of your health-care provider, it is worth looking into to see if you can take advantage of an HSA. If you are paying for your own health care, it is a no-brainer to take advantage of this system. It saves on taxes and helps you build wealth for inevitable medical expenses.

17

Roth IRA, Little Known Facts

Roth IRAs have value as a tax-free vessel for your retirement money, and they have a hidden benefit that very few people know about. The principal you use to fund your Roth IRA can be taken out and used to pay for college tuition without any penalties or taxes (not earnings or interest).

Let's see what kind of numbers you could have if you start funding a Roth IRA at the age of eighteen. If you religiously contribute the maximum amount of $5,000 per year, in twenty-five years, you will have deposited $125,000 of principal. For twenty-four years, you have been compounding the interest on that $125,000. You now will be forty-three years old and could easily have a child who is ready for college. You could, in theory, use that $125,000 to pay for your child's higher education—while still having a goose laying a golden egg in your Roth IRA—since you can't touch the interest or earnings, and the compound interest machine is still earning interest on your dividends.

You won't take all the principal out at once. In the next four or five years, you will be adding another $20,000 to $25,000 of principal to the account. This can be a supplement to help pay for college rather than the main way to send your kids to college.

Many people are not disciplined enough to make this benefit work as a goal to get a retirement account *and* fund your children's college tuitions. However, this could be a tremendous addition to any other savings you set aside for higher education. If you keep this information in mind, it may help with expenses down the road—along with a compound interest benefit.

A 529 savings plan is another good way to set aside money for higher education.

18

Caring for Aging Parents

Baby boomers are one of the largest segments of society. We are postured to be one of the wealthiest generations the world has ever seen. Baby boomers are spenders, which is really good for consumer economics: high-priced cars, second homes, and lavish vacations. It sounds like a bright economic future thanks to the passing of the previous generation, but as responsible sons and daughters, we must be sure our parents are cared for in their final days. This can be a very painful subject, and many people do not want to face it.

My three siblings and I were unified in our handling of our aging parents. My parents wanted us to learn, succeed, and share that knowledge with others who wanted and needed help. They ascribed to the thought that giving a man a fish will feed him for a day and teaching a man to fish will feed him for life. This model for generating an income stream that can be used for whatever needs you have played out to the very end of their lives.

My parents got it all—just the way they planned. Prior to

my father becoming ill, he made sure we knew his wishes if he were incapacitated. If he was on a machine that kept him alive, he wanted us to pull the plug. If anything happened to him, I was to take over the finances for my mother—even though my eldest sister was the executor of my parents' estate. This was not a reflection of her ability; instead, he was dividing the responsibility to whoever was best suited for a particular task. Since I worked closely with my father on our investment model, he decided I would know his investments the best. My father was ill for a very brief time before passing, and there was no pain or suffering. Because he had a will in place, things moved very quickly to my mother. Things never missed a beat thanks to their prior planning.

My father had 100 percent of his investments in high-yield stocks. Almost all financial planners would totally disagree with this idea. I only made two changes to my father's investments. I moved his account to a discount brokerage account where I could make purchases on my mother's behalf without the high brokerage fees. My father liked calling a broker to make purchases and sales, but those fees were way too high for me. My father never wanted to do trading by a computer.

He kept very little cash reserve in his stock account, and almost every dividend he received was reinvested. In his mind, that was no problem because he handled all of my parents' finances, including paying bills and grocery shopping. We thought there was not enough cash in reserve for an emergency. After much thought about what emergencies could arise, we determined an amount that should be held in reserve for the immediate needs of our mother and any unknown needs that could pop up. We held back part of the monthly dividends in cash and reinvested part in the investment model. Things went along seamlessly for my mother because of my parents' prior planning. Please don't let your parents wait until it is too late to have at least a will for each of them.

After a year or so, my accountant became the executor to his brother's estate. His brother had fifty-nine rental properties, no will, and an estranged wife and son. It was a complete nightmare for my friend. He suggested that my mother should consider a trust for her estate so that we would have an extra veil of protection and avoid probate court, which could tie up assets for months or years if there was any contesting of her will. He said, "When money or things are involved, it does strange things to people—even people you might never expect to act adversely."

We made the decision, with my mother's approval, to put all her assets in a trust along with a new will to support her trust. My mother lived for five years after my father passed away, and her ending was not nearly as short as my father's. Early in the year of her death, she was diagnosed with a terminal illness that would require continuous chemotherapy. After one treatment she made the choice to not continue the painful treatments. She also did not want to spend her last days at home. She made that point very clear.

The only solution was to place her in hospice care, which we did. She spent that entire year in hospice. Because of father's vision for creating an income stream for his family, all his planning played out to a winning formula. My mother's bills were completely covered every month by her income from investments *without* touching any of the principal.

During that time, knowing the amount we would need each

month, I made adjustments on two of my father's high-yield stocks. I sold two of the holdings that were paying 5–7 percent and replaced them with more volatile stocks that were paying 12–17 percent. Having cash every month was more important than the value of the stock.

My siblings and I were left with a trust account that was pretty much intact—despite the large hospice bills that needed to be paid from that account every month. Although it turned out to be just as our parents wanted, we were totally prepared to liquidate all of the trust assets to provide care for our mother. My father's vision put us in a very comfortable position during a very uncomfortable situation. If you take the time and effort to prepare for the future, many bad situations can be softened or avoided. Money is the sharpest and most versatile tool in your toolbox.

19

Retirement Income Trust

Most parents would like to be able to leave their children something in the way of wealth to help them avoid or soften the struggles in life. Warren Buffett was asked what he was going to leave his children in the way of an inheritance. He said, "I want to leave them enough that they do something, but not so much that they do nothing." That statement speaks of love, caring, responsibility, and good stewardship.

I recently discovered retirement income trust, which is an insurance annuity with a one-time single premium of around $8,000 that can grow to about $500,000 in fifty years. This premium/policy has to be put into a trust to prevent the beneficiary from touching it or altering it until maturity at the age of sixty-five. What a great way to create generational wealth for a family heritage! For less than $10,000, your children and grandchildren can have a tremendous legacy that can continue for generations. Compounding interest can generate great amounts of wealth.

20

Make Your Children Millionaires... Sooner Rather Than Later

The retirement income trust is really an outstanding concept, but like all insurance policies, the one that makes the most money is the insurance companies (and the agent that sell you the policy). I have come up with a great concept for anyone who has vision for the future and wants to help their family's future generations.

This information may be frustrating for readers. It is hard enough to save for yourself—let alone for another family member—but I want to plant this seed because it could be life changing for you or someone you care about. Prior to discovering the retirement income trust, my wife and I started a savings program for our granddaughter. We wanted to contribute to her life, her future, and her well-being in a more meaningful way than buying things for her that have little shelf life or toys that are played with for a short period and then sit in a toy box or end up being sold at a yard sale.

We opened a stock brokerage account in her name with

our son's name and Social Security number. That allowed a minor child to own and trade stocks and securities. The program for this is the Uniform Gifts to Minors Act (UGMA), but it leaves my son in total control of what happens with the account. He will maintain control of that account until her eighteenth birthday. On her eighteenth birthday, the account automatically becomes her account. This is something that both my son and I do not want!

Before her eighteenth birthday, we will take her name off of the account since we don't want to hand over a large amount of money to an eighteen-year-old—regardless of all the coaching we may give her. The last thing we want is for her to come home one day and show her parents the new Porsche she just bought. We both feel this account should be left in my son's control until she demonstrates that she knows how it works and how to handle it before handing her the reins.

In example 1, you will see an annual contribution from birth until age eighteen (which is actually nineteen years of contributions). The tax implications on the earnings are not included in this example. Like most parents, our son will include this account's 1099 on his personal tax return and not worry about her account paying those taxes. At age eighteen, that account will have a tax liability under current tax laws. With 15 percent tax on unearned income, dividend, the tax due will be around $1,141.24. Even at only 15 percent tax liability, that is still a substantial amount of money to hand over to Uncle Sam in a lump sum.

We can apply another example here. After she turns eighteen, we can hold back some of the dividends in cash reserve to pay for the upcoming tax liability. The account will generate approximately $634 per month in dividends, and we will set aside a small amount of the dividends each month in cash to pay the tax on the account's earnings. The success of this model depends on reinvesting as much of the dividends as possible to keep that compound snowball growing.

In example 1, we illustrate what happens if these principles are enforced. A $500 annual contribution nets over $50,000 for a total contribution of $9,500 in just nineteen years, which is almost 23 percent compound interest. After age eighteen (nineteen years) with no $500 annual contribution—just reinvesting the monthly dividends until age forty—my granddaughter will have over $1 million in savings from my total contribution of only $9,500. This model beats the retirement income trust by double, in less than half the time, with no insurance company or trust lawyer.

It all happens through the power of compound interest. The maintenance of this plan to keep it going once it is in place is minutes per month. The most work required for this plan and all other model examples in this book will be finding investment stocks that you will want to add as your investment nest egg gets larger and larger.

Example # 1

(1) $500.00 X .15 = $575.00
(2) $575.00 + $500.00 X .15 = $1,236.25
(3) $1,236.25 + $500.00 X .15 = $1,996.69
(4) $1,996.69 + $500.00 X .15 = $2,871.19
(5) $2,871.19 + $500.00 X .15 = $3,876.87
(6) $3,876.87 + $500.00 X .15 = $5,033.40
(7) $5,033.40 + $500.00 X .15 = $6,363.41
(8) $6,363.41 + $500.00 X .15 = $7,892.93
(9) $7,892.93 + $500.00 X .15 = $9,651.86
(10) $9,651.86 + $500.00 X .15 = $11,674.69
(11) $11,674.69 + 500.00 X .15 = $14,000.84
(12) $14,000.84 + $500.00 X .15 = $16,676.00
(13) $16,676.00 + $500.00 X .15 = $19,752.36
(14) $19,752.36 + $500.00 X .15 = $23,290.21
(15) $23,290.21 + $500.00 X .15 = $27,358.74
(16) $27,358.74 + $500.00 X .15 = $32,037.55
(17) $32,037.55 + $500.00 X .15 = $37,418.19
(18) $37,418.19 + $500.00 X .15 = $43,605.91
(19) $43,607.91 + $500.00 X .15 = $50,721.80
18 YEARS OLD

TOTAL CONTRIBUTION $500.00 X 19 YEARS
= $9,500.00
  $41,221.80 EARNINGS
  23% COMPOUND INTEREST
NO CONTRIBUTIONS AFTER 18 YEARS OLD

(20) $50,721.80 X 1.15 = $58,330.17
(21) $58,330.17 X 1.15 = $67,079.58
(22) $67,079.58 X 1.15 = $77,141.52
(23) $77,141.52 X 1.15 = $88,712.74
(24) $88,712.74 X 1.15 = $102,019.65
(25) $102,019.65 X 1.15 = $117,322.59
(26) $117,322.59 X 1.15 = $134,920.97
(27) $134,920.97 X 1.15 = $155,159.11
(28) $155,159.11 X 1.15 = $178,432.97
(29) $178,432.97 X 1.15 = $205,197.91
(30) $205,197.91 X 1.15 = $235,977.59
(31) $235,977.59 X 1.15 = $271,374.22
(32) $271,374.22 X 1.15 = $312,080.35
(33) $312,080.35 X 1.15 = $358,892.40
(34) $358,892.40 X 1.15 = $412,726.26
(35) $412,726.26 X 1.15 = $474,635.19
(36) $474,635.19 X 1.15 = $545,830.46
(37) $545,830.46 X 1.15 = $627,705.02
(38) $627,705.02 X 1.15 = $721,860.77
(39) $721,860.77 X 1.15 = $830,139.88
(40) $830,139.88 X 1.15 = $954,660.86
(41) $954,660.86 X 1.15 = $1,097,859.90
40 YEARS OLD

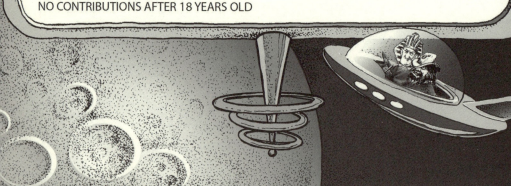

Let's look at how compound interest really snowballs when the initial investment seed is larger. This comparison is closer to the retirement income trust. In example 2, I used the amount that will be contributed to my granddaughter's account as the lump sum seed amount. Take a look at what happens with a larger starting amount (using my same 15 percent ROI model). By the age of forty, this will be within a stone's throw of $3 million. That is six times the amount projected by retirement income trust of $500,000 at age sixty-five—and it is twenty-five years earlier.

Example # 2

ONE TIME DEPOSIT OF $9,500

(1) $9,500.00 X 1.15 = $10,925.00
(2) $10,925.00 X 1.15 = $12,563.75
(3) $12,563.75 X 1.15 = $14,448.31
(4) $14,448.31 X 1.15 = $16,615.56
(5) $16,615.56 X 1.15 = $19,107.89
(6) $19,107.89 X 1.15 = $21,974.07
(7) $21,974.07 X 1.15 = $25,270.19
(8) $25,270.19 X 1.15 = $29,060.71
(9) $29,060.71 X 1.15 = $33,419.82
(10) $33,419.82 X 1.15 = $38,432.79
(11) $38,432.79 X 1.15 = $44,197.71
(12) $44,197.71 X 1.15 = $50,827.36
(13) $50,827.36 X 1.15 = $58,451.47
(14) $58,451.47 X 1.15 = $67,219.19
(15) $67,219.19 X 1.15 = $77,302.07
(16) $77,302.07 X 1.15 = $88,897.38
(17) $88,897.38 X 1.15 = $102,232.00
(18) $102,232.00 X 1.15 = 117,566.77
(19) $117,566.77 X 1.15 = $135,201.78
(20) $135,201.78 X 1.15 = $155,482.04
(21) $155,482.04 X 1.15 = $178,804.34

(22) $178,804.34 X 1.15 = $205,625.00
(23) $205,625.00 X 1.15 = $236,468.73
(24) $236,468.73 X 1.15 = $271,939.00
(25) $271,939.00 X 1.15 = $312,729.88
(26) $312,729.88 X 1.15 = $359,639.36
(27) $359,639.36 X 1.15 = $413,585.26
(28) $413,585.26 X 1.15 = $475,623.00
(29) $475,623.00 X 1.15 = $549,966.49
(30) $549,966.49 X 1.15 = $629,011.46
(31) $629,011.46 X 1.15 = $723,363.17
(32) $723,363.17 X 1.15 = $831,867.64
(33) $831,867.64 X 1.15 = $956,647.78
(34) $956,647.78 X 1.15 = $1,100,144.90
(35) $1,100,144.90 X 1.15 = $1,265,166.60
(36) $1,265,166.60 X 1.15 = $1,454,941.50
(37) $1,454,941.50 X 1.15 = $1,673,182.70
(38) $1,673,182.70 X 1.15 = $1,924,160.00
(39) $1,924,160.00 X 1.15 = $2,212,784.00
(40) $2,212,784.00 X 1.15 = $2,544,701.70
(41) $2,544,701.70 X 1.15 = $2,926,406.90

$2,926,406.90 BY THE AGE OF 40

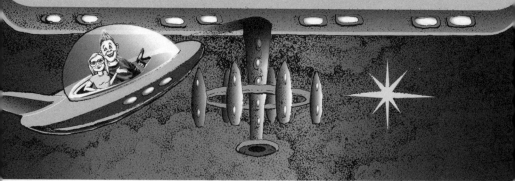

Just for fun, let's see what happens if we take it out to age sixty-five. Example 3 shows my 15 percent investment model from age forty-two to sixty-five, and the principal goes from a little over $3 million to almost $84 million in twenty-four years.

Shocking, isn't it!

By now, you have an idea that the compound interest principles are almost magic, but seeing it carried out in print makes a very dramatic statement. That is why Albert Einstein indicated that compound interest was one of the most powerful forces in the universe. He said that compound interest is the eighth wonder of the world.

You may look at these examples and think there is no way you can do this—even if you come up with the seed money to start it. How can it keep it going at this pace? Is this 15 percent return even possible?

Example

3

(42) \$2,926,406.90 X 1.15 = \$3,365,367.90
(43) \$3,365,367.90 X 1.15 = \$3,870,173.00
(44) \$3,870,173.00 X 1.15 = \$4,450,698.90
(45) \$4,450,698.90 X 1.15 = \$5,118,303.70
(46) \$5,118,303.70 X 1.15 = \$5,886,049.20
(47) \$5,886,049.20 X 1.15 = \$6,768,956.50
(48) \$6,768,956.50 X 1.15 = \$7,784,299.90
(49) \$7,784,299.90 X 1.15 = \$8,951,944.80
(50) \$8,951,944.80 X 1.15 = \$10,294,736.00
(51) \$10,294,736.00 X 1.15 = \$11,838,946.00
(52) \$11,838,946.00 X 1.15 = \$13,614,787.00
(53) \$13,614,787.00 X 1.15 = \$15,657,005.00
(54) \$15,657,005.00 X 1.15 = \$18,005,555.00
(55) \$18,005,555.00 X 1.15 = \$20,706,388.00
(56) \$20,706,388.00 X 1.15 = \$23,812,346.00
(57) \$23,812,346.00 X 1.15 = \$27,384,197.00
(58) \$27,384,197.00 X 1.15 = \$31,491,826.00
(59) \$31,491,826.00 X 1.15 = \$36,215,599.00
(60) \$36,215,599.00 X 1.15 = \$41,647,938.00
(61) \$41,647,938.00 X 1.15 = \$47,895,128.00
(62) \$47,895,128.00 X 1.15 = \$55,079,397.00
(63) \$55,079,397.00 X 1.15 = \$63,341,306.00
(64) \$63,341,306.00 X 1.15 = \$72,842,501.00
(65) \$72,842,501.00 X 1.15 = \$83,768,876.00

When I first started looking into how compound interest worked, it was not very impressive. When you start with small amounts, the realized returns do not appear to be all that much. However, you are earning interest on your interest, which is somewhat silent and a little sneaky. This can have the opposite effect if you are paying interest on your interest via unpaid credit card balances. It can appear to be not all that much.

Einstein said, "Those who understand compound interest earn it—those who don't pay it."

I am here to tell you it is big! It is bigger than big! It is huge! And you can do it. Let me offer a comparison in nature. The great redwood tree is mammoth. Some trees are over three hundred feet in height and more than a thousand years old, but they all start out from a single seed. Your stock savings can grow to the scale of a redwood tree if you start the seed and keep it growing. It can grow to an enormous size with very little attention by simply putting your dividends back in to your investment model.

Here is a real-life example of monstrous compound interest. One of our greatest founding fathers was Benjamin Franklin. Ben Franklin completely understood the power of compound interest. Late in his life, he put his understanding of compound interest and love for his fellow man to work by providing a trust for the cities of Boston and Philadelphia. The seed money for these trusts in today's money was about $4,500 for each city. The stipulation was this money must remain invested for one hundred years before they could access a portion of funds—and then complete access to the balance came after two hundred years. By the time the two hundred years arrived, Boston's trust was worth more than half a billion dollars, which is not bad for a $4,500 commitment.

Compound interest is one of the great rules of mathematics. It is a law of nature that will work for you no matter who you are. No matter what your background is, if you choose to use it, it will work for you. It is guaranteed. Electricity is very similar to compound interest because it is a part of the natural order of things. It is available for our use, but we need to use it wisely. If we don't use it properly, it can hurt us. Be wise. These rules exist, and we can benefit if we choose to make use of them. It is your choice.

These examples display numbers growing to enormous proportion, which makes it hard to believe there is anything out there to invest in that can support that kind of growth. There are many high-yield garden-variety stocks out there to choose from. You may have to look at many before picking any that you feel comfortable putting your money into, and that is okay. Don't be discouraged. I continue to look at hundreds of stocks before I end up with one or two I like or consider buying. The best resource today is using the web to search for high-yield stocks. The choices will be overwhelming, but they are easy to eliminate. I look at three aspects before purchasing:

- at least 9 percent in cash dividends annually
- a history of paying high yields
- which industry they are in

That is it. It is pretty simple and straightforward. It is not very sexy, but I want reliable, steadfast, and consistent cash that I can put back into my model to keep that snowball growing. Even if I want some of the cash for other things, I don't have to sell stock to make that happen. This way, I can have both.

This simple formula will facilitate your nest egg into the millions of dollars without changing your investment selections. If you are diligent and your returns annually grow to more than a million (which they will if you stick to this plan), you will need to look for additional investments that net 15 percent and greater.

With larger amounts to invest, new doors for investment products will open. Hedge funds are the first thing that comes to mind. A hedge fund is a pool of capital in limited partnership that is directed by a manager or a group of managers who use various techniques to make their selections grow. The minimum to get into one of these funds is usually $100,000, but they can go as high as $1 million for having the privilege of managers investing their clients' money. The fees for this service may be 1 percent or 2 percent of the money invested plus 20 percent of the earnings. Just like annuities, the people who are making out the best are the people who sell you their products or services.

Another potential high-yield investment is often offered by developers who use outside investors to fund their projects, generally with a 20 percent ROI and a relatively safe investment. They may require a million-dollar minimum to invest for the duration of construction and then pay back the investor principal and interest once the project is completed. The developer will have cash flowing in or get conventional financing if they want to take more money out of the project. This is nothing new and has been done for years. You need to lay out a lot of money in order to make a lot of money. That is how the rich get richer.

No one will look out for your money like you do. Stick to the garden-variety high-yield stocks, and you will get your millions. After that, should you be fortunate enough to have excess money, give me a call—and I will help you find something solid to invest in.

PART 5

Want More... Give More!

21

Tithing, A Promise For Prosperity

Early in my professional career, I took an interest in successful icons of industry. I began looking for common threads for their success. What was the driving force or motivation that made them hop out of bed and go right to the day's tasks? From the very first blush, an easy answer could be money. Money or the lack thereof was often an element to their stories. Andrew Carnegie mentioned how his first investment turned his attention to making money without physically working for it. He was making ten cents an hour as a porter for the Pennsylvania Railroad at fourteen years old. The company allowed employees to buy stock in the company. He saved some money and bought some stock. When the stock paid a dividend, it paid him more than his hourly rate. The revelation that came to him was that he didn't have to work for that money. That was what it took to get going to get money.

Walt Disney and Milton Hershey were leaders who created their own paths, and I revere them both. Both men had tremendous success—but only after tremendous failures.

Despite the financial failures and setbacks, they had an energy or a spirit in their core that made them keep trying to fulfill their destinies. If you study many of history's great business leaders and icons, you will see the desire for financial gratification, but you will also notice that money is secondary to their dreams and goals. For the most part, once these leaders realize they have made an impact on the world—and the world has rewarded them for their efforts—they begin to focus part of their efforts on giving back.

What is the force that causes selected individuals to go after visions, achievements, and goals? They recognize something from within that directs them to keep looking and trying until something clicks into place. We all have it. We are born with it. The ones who dig for it, pursue it, and then uncover it are the ones who love what they are doing. They are the ones who will work on what they are doing and not watch the clock. They don't know what time it is, and many times, they don't care.

In many cases, they aren't even getting paid. It may even be costing them money, but there is something inside. An idea or a vision has to come out. At first, failure may be their only reward. That is unacceptable to them, and they will keep at it until success is achieved. History holds countless accounts of such achievements. We all have this inside. There are things that resonates with us when we see, hear, touch, taste, or smell them. It excites us, and it jars our minds. It throws us back in time to where memories play movies for us.

Our five senses are all connected. Motivation helps make us who we are. Our core spirit is the driving force that leads to our passions, likes, dislikes, and the drive that manifests into accomplishments and achievements. Every person who has walked this earth is born with a unique skill set that can provide for their needs and benefit others. So many achievements occurred because someone was motivated with an idea they wanted to see come to be. Where does this spirit come from? What is this energy? That energy or that spirit lives in all of us, and it was a creation of God!

If you are not a believer, I can prove His presence in a factual manner and leave it up to you to come up with your own conclusions. Let me start with where we live. Earth is one planet that gives all the elements we need to support life. The earth's location in our solar system is just at the right distance from the sun so that life can exist. It rotates around the sun once a year so that we have four seasons. These orderly elements are in place and allow us to exist.

What is gravity? A law of nature? It keeps the planets in the locations they are supposed to be in. It keeps the moon at the proper distance from the earth. Gravity keeps us on the ground, and it causes an apple to fall from a tree. Sir Isaac Newton pointed that out to us.

What is electricity? It is an energy that we harness to do things for us. Benjamin Franklin pointed that out to us. We live in a world of order, rules of nature, and laws of the universe that we have no control over. We do not have the ability to change them. It does not matter if you are a good person or a bad person, a believer or a nonbeliever, if you fall off a building, you will hit the ground. Nothing we can do will change that.

All the elements of our universe, planet, and social order have finite laws that have perfect order. They are in place and assist us in existence. To take it a step further, there is mathematical order and rules that help us design, create, and solve problems. All these specifications are interlaced and work harmoniously without any assistance from humankind. We have calculated the time the sun rises every day of the year perfectly, precisely, and without error.

Have the rules, laws, and conditions that control all the elements that support life just happened by chance? As a young boy, we were studying the constellations in school and trying to find them in the sky. I was wondering how they got there and what kept them in place. If you reach the edge of our universe, what is on the other side? What put all those stars in place and kept them there? When did that happen? Why did that happen? Many ancient societies and cultures have looked at the same things, asked the very same questions, and observed the natural orders. They almost always came to the same conclusion: someone or something great put this together.

What does this have to do with high-yield investing? Stick with me—and you will see. Early man recognized all these laws and order of nature. There are other laws of nature that apply to the nature of man that are behavioral: how we work together, how we treat each other, and the consequences for our actions toward one another. Here are a few that come to mind. You reap what you sow relates to rewards for work. If you live by the sword, you will die by the sword relates to the violent treatment of others and the consequences that will be your fate for such treatment of others. What goes around comes around relates to how gossiping about others will come back to you in an embarrassing way. One of my favorites is you can never give kindness away—it will always come back to you.

These behavioral laws and many other universal laws happen between people regardless of your beliefs. A great deal of belief has to do with the makeup of humans, the societal creatures we are, and how we perceive ourselves. There are actions for our treatment of others. They may not be immediate, but there are consequences for our actions.

The greatest wealth builder is the mathematical principle of compound interest. The laws of mathematics work and are as finite as the laws of gravity. They affect everyone regardless of who you are. If you look at all the rules that direct us, guide us, and affect what we can and cannot do, you may wonder how all this came together. Is this orderliness by chance?

Orderliness comes from something that has been well thought out. The orderliness that governs humankind comes from a supreme being, an expert in design and planning, an artist of the highest perfection. The beauty and wonders of nature are the works of God. My last principle for building and maximizing your wealth comes directly from God. It is a rule that has cause and effect like gravity, electricity, mathematics, and His Word promises it. God specifically challenged us to test Him on this principle. That other wealth-generating principle is tithing.

Tithing is the practice of giving back to God 10 percent of your earnings—the first 10 percent, your best! For most of my spiritual walk, I have understood tithing, but it has really come to an enlightened height through my research and studies for writing this book. In my quest for more real-life information that supports God's work, I came across a tiny little publication called the *Guidepost*. I read a powerful article about tithing. I was so excited that I contacted the *Guidepost* to see if I could reach out to the author. They were very cooperative and gave me the author's contact information. To my shock and delight, the author was a neighbor of mine. I felt great excitement about finding this great resource in my own backyard. I contacted Harry Donovan, and it was very clear that he understood and practiced the principles of tithing and was a man of God. After talking about his article, my excitement continued to grow. He had a wealth of information from years of empirical knowledge and formal education.

At the end of our conversation, I asked Harry if he would allow me to interview him about his life's journey and how tithing fit into his life so completely. This brief story about Harry Donovan will help me explain trust in God and honoring Him through His Word, which includes tithing as a model for a bountiful life.

When Harry was about eleven years old, he earned some money by working at a grocery store. He proudly showed his mother the money he had earned, and she praised him for his accomplishment—and then she directed him to give the first 10 percent to God. She explained to him that was called tithing. That stuck with Harry for his entire life.

Throughout his life and career, he put his love for God first, and it showed in the guidance he gave others. After Harry served in World War II under General MacArthur, he came home, earned a degree, and became a CPA. His mission to help people continued, and tithing was a part of how he helped people understand the greatness of God's role in his personal life.

When I shared my plans for this book, he asked about its theme.

I explained how it was based on my success in high-yield

investing, the miracle of compound interest, and how the investment model included God and tithing.

He said, "Would you mind if I read it?"

"Of course! I would be honored!" I replied.

The next time we got together, he praised my writing, endorsed the content, and encouraged me to finish it because it would help a lot of people who are looking for direction on these topics. We became friends and talked periodically, and I asked for his permission to include him on the tithing section of this book.

With his blessing and some of his published material, I was able to expand my knowledge of his advocacy of tithing. I will never get to let Harry know how much of a positive impact he made on me with the kindness, wisdom, and generosity he shared with others. He was generous with his time and money. We agree that time is the most precious possession of all since all the money in the world cannot buy more time.

Harry passed away before I was finished writing this book. He was ninety years old. As a strong advocate for tithing, he believed in challenging people he knew very well to commit to tithing for a year. If, at the end of that year, their finances were not as improved as expected, he would match their money set aside to give to God. He made this offer to several people throughout his career as a CPA, and not one person took him up on his offer because the results were always as God promised.

The promise Harry is speaking of comes from Malachi 3:10. "Bring all the tithes into the store house so that there will be food enough in My temple; if you do, I will open up the windows of heaven for you and pour out a blessing so great you won't have room enough to take it in! Try it! Let Me prove it to you!"

This is a strong point for those who believe the Word of God. Harry lived the principles of his beliefs and was rewarded for it. He shared it with all who wanted to hear what he had to say.

At this point, I would like to address the nonbelievers, the doubters, and more secular-minded people. Think about giving in relationship to investing and accruing wealth from it. Let's look at the benefits of giving as a rule of nature or even the natural order of things in society. What is the feeling you get when you give someone something or do something kind for someone you know—or someone you don't know? When you do something or give something to someone you don't know, the feeling is even more intense. What is that feeling? I am going to call it joy. Have you ever done something for someone that brought tears of joy to their eyes or even made them cry? For me, that is one of the greatest rushes of all.

People say, "It is better to give than to receive," and that cliché is spot-on accurate. Have you ever noticed how happy a generous person is and how grumpy a stingy, self-centered person is? Start making note of happy people versus grumpy people, and I think you will see a correlation with happiness and giving.

For me, giving comes in three forms: time, treasure, (money), and talent. These are all possessions that we can donate to someone or to an organization in need. All have value, and all are worthy in society. Time is the thing I give most sparingly because if I waste it, I can't get any more to replace it.

The treasure—money—is the universal element. Just as we learned in sixth-grade science class that water is the universal solvent, money can do more tasks than any of the others because of its universal acceptance. It is the sharpest tool in your toolbox.

Talent is passing on the years of knowledge and experience to those who can benefit from your expertise. Keeping these things in mind and in your plans for investing, another rule of nature (or mathematics) elevates your cause for a balanced model and a way to build wealth. This scripture is one of the most powerful writings I have ever read because God challenges us to test Him on His Word. I am not a theologian, but in all my studies, I cannot recall anywhere else in the Bible where God challenges us to test Him.

Harry Donovan lived his whole life honoring God with this in mind, and if you were to ask him about his blessings, he would say that they all came from God—and his tithing was in obedience and Honor to God. Giving is such an important part of our existence here on earth, and whether you believe as I do, or not, everything is from God.

The effects of being a giver will have an impact on the one receiving the gift and to you, the one who provides the gift. It is not whether you tithe or not—tithing is not a magic pill that will make everything perfect or eliminate all your money problems. What is most important is giving based on what is in your heart. Giving cheerfully creates the joy that only comes from giving. If the heart is begrudging, the giver really gets nothing out of the act of giving except a troubled heart.

If the 10 percent giving outlined in my money management model is not comfortable, adjust it to your comfort level. If you do it with a positive, joyful heart, the results will be the same as if you adhere to 10 percent. Your act of giving will not go unnoticed. The simple model I have outlined has been developed to help the average person take total control of their finances so that they can provide a good quality of life for themselves and their families—through balance.

In my quest for success, many things became unbalanced, causing strife, which is contrary to joy, and joy is an important element for balance and success. I have uncovered some gold nuggets in my quest for proof of my beliefs. I have been studying King Solomon, the son of David (Remember the story of David & Goliath?). King Solomon is said to have been the wealthiest man to have ever lived ever—even wealthier than Warren Buffett or Bill Gates. He came into all his wealth because he asked God for wisdom.

Solomon is also credited with being the wisest man to have ever lived. Solomon wisely points out that riches mean much more than money. "It is possible to give away and become richer! It is also possible to hold on too tightly and lose everything. Yes, the liberal man shall be rich! By watering others, he waters himself" (Proverbs 11:24).